English Here and There
読解と基本文法で極める総合英語

Terry O'Brien
Kei Mihara
Tadashi Enya
Hiroshi Kimura

NAN'UN-DO

はしがき

「今日の授業はよくわかった、得るものがあった、楽しかった」と受講生が満ち足りた気持ちで教室から出て行くなら、それは主体的・協働的な学びであったと言えるでしょう。授業展開で受ける刺激が同じであれば、だんだん飽きてしまいます。逆に言えば、刺激を変えれば飽きないということです。良い授業では「変化」をつける工夫が求められます。そうすることで受講生は飽きる前に次の学習に移れます。この教材は「飽きさせない」ことに配慮した30ユニットで構成され、授業に「変化」を持たせることができます。つまり、形式の異なる奇数・偶数ユニットに取り組むことで、学びのスイッチを切り替えることができるのです。

本書は、日常の身近なトピックを題材にした親しみやすい初級・準中級レベルの英語総合教材です。ストーリーを中心に、各種エクササイズに取り組みながら、日常生活で求められる英語力を身につけることができます。また、バラエティーに富んだトピックから、いろんなシチュエーションで使われる基本語彙を定着させることができます。

本書のストーリーは、車の運転、バスや電車での移動、買い物など、誰もが日常的に経験するトピックについて、ちょっとしたエピソードを交え、おもしろく書かれています。写真やイラストを使った問題を解いたり、ストーリーを読んだり、リスニングやライティング、文法などの問題を解いたりしてください。そして、会話文は聞くだけでなく、実際に発音して、表現を覚えてください。そうすることによって、読んだり聞いたりというインプット・スキルに加え、書いたり話したりというアウトプット・スキルも向上します。

本書の特長

1. 授業形態に応じた工夫が可能な30ユニット
2. 文法に配慮した200語程度の英文エッセイでリーディング力を強化
3. さまざまな練習問題で内容理解度を確認
4. 英文を完成することでライティング力を習得
5. 60語程度の会話でリスニング力を強化
6. イラストや写真の説明文の単語を考えることで語彙力を増強

本書を通じて、基礎をしっかり固め、総合的な英語力を楽しく無理なく身につけていただければ幸いです。

2020年春
著者

Download Audio
音声ファイル
無料DL
のご案内

このテキストの音声を無料で視聴（ストリーミング）・ダウンロードできます。自習用音声としてご活用ください。
以下のサイトにアクセスしてテキスト番号で検索してください。

https://nanun-do.com　テキスト番号［**512047**］

※無線LAN（WiFi）に接続してのご利用を推奨いたします。

※音声ダウンロードはZipファイルでの提供になります。
お使いの機器によっては別途ソフトウェア（アプリケーション）の導入が必要となります。

本書の使い方

全体で 30 ユニットです。奇数ユニットと偶数ユニットで形式が異なります。どちらもストーリーと会話を中心に写真やイラスト問題を含めて、基本的な英語力を伸ばせるような構成になっています。

テキストの使い方については、授業形態によって、いろいろ工夫ができます。どのユニットからでも始められます。

1. 2 つのユニット（奇数・偶数ユニット）を授業時間内に行う。
2. 奇数ユニットは授業で使い、偶数ユニットは家庭学習の課題とする（またはその逆)。

［奇数ユニット］

Warm-up

写真やイラストを説明するため、英文の空所に与えられた文字で始まる単語を書きます。

1 Reading

1 文法問題で空所に単語を補充します。

2 指示に従って単語を変えたり、英文を書き換えたりします。

3 内容理解度の確認のため、代名詞が何を指しているかを答えます。

4 本文の内容に合うように空所に入る単語を書きます。

5 アクセント問題や発音問題があります。

6 語句の並べ替え問題があります。

2 Conversation

A 日本文を参考にして空所内の語句を並べ替えます。

B 次に **A** の英文を適切な空所に入れて会話を完成します。

C 質問に対する正しい答えを (A) (B) から選びます。

［偶数ユニット］

1 Reading

1 文中の単語の意味を選びます。

2 英文が本文の内容に合っていれば T、違っていれば F を選びます。

2 Conversation

A 会話を聞いて空所に単語を書きます。

B 質問を聞いて空所に単語を書き、適切な答えを (A) (B) から選びます。

3 Short Talk

イラストを見ながら、空所に入る単語を語群より選び、文章を完成させます。

教科書の付属音声について

学習者用ダウンロード音声　https://www.nanun-do.com より音声をダウンロードできます。

教授者用音声 CD　教授者用の教室用 CD 音声を用意しています。

Contents

Unit 1	Our Garden　be 動詞 花壇の見学はバスで	6
Unit 2	Do you trust your GPS? ジーピーエスの過信は禁物	9
Unit 3	The History of the Village　一般動詞 村の変遷の歴史	11
Unit 4	Waiting for a Plane 空港待合室の若者	14
Unit 5	Where are my socks?　代名詞 ソックスがどこかへ！	16
Unit 6	Are you all right? 買い物帰りに転倒	19
Unit 7	Checking in at a Hotel　数詞 観光バスがホテルに到着	21
Unit 8	Tour Schedule 明日の観光予定は・・・	24
Unit 9	House for Sale　前置詞・接続詞 少し価格の高い売り物件	26
Unit 10	The City 都市のモールで買い物	29
Unit 11	Our Company　助動詞・完了形 会社を案内	31
Unit 12	At the Hospital 病院で一晩容態の観察	34
Unit 13	Packing Your Bags　関係代名詞・命令文 海外旅行の荷造りアドバイス	36
Unit 14	A Train Ticket 国によって異なる切符の買い方	39
Unit 15	Airport Forms　関係副詞 空港での用紙の記入方法	41

Unit 16 **During the Flight** 44
必要なものは手元に

Unit 17 **What kind of person?** 不定詞・動名詞 46
第一印象が良い！

Unit 18 **At the Hotel** 49
ホテルの部屋の苦情

Unit 19 **Driving Instructions** 形容詞・副詞 51
オートマチック車の運転

Unit 20 **A Lovely Blouse** 54
すてきなブラウスの購入

Unit 21 **How was your room?** 疑問詞・未来形 56
ホテルの部屋に関する質問

Unit 22 **What happened?** 59
車の衝突事故

Unit 23 **Shopping** 可算名詞・不可算名詞 61
食事の準備に必要なもの

Unit 24 **Street Directions** 64
銀行への道順

Unit 25 **My Luxury** there 構文・使役動詞 66
贅沢な過ごし方とは？

Unit 26 **A Tall Young Man** 69
よく学ぶ背の高い学生

Unit 27 **Reading Your Mind** 進行形・現在分詞 71
避けたい他人を傷つける言葉！

Unit 28 **I lost my camera.** 74
駅でカメラを紛失

Unit 29 **In the Police Box** 受動態・仮定法 76
迷子になった祖母の説明

Unit 30 **Studying English** 79
英語を学ぶ最善の方法とは？

Unit 1 Our Garden　be 動詞

Warm-up

次の日本語を参考にして、空所に与えられた文字で始まる単語を書きなさい。

枝　　肥料　　日光　　引き抜く

1. You should look after your garden. Your garden needs (s　　　　　　　), water, and (f　　　　　　　).
2. You should (p　　　　　　) up the weeds and cut the long (b　　　　　　) of the trees.

1 Reading

CD 02

[1]My house is in the country. [2]It is an old house. It has a large flower garden. My dad wasn't happy working in the factory, so he took an early retirement, and now he spends every day in the fresh air. Can you see the man standing over there near the gate? [3]That is my father. He looks after the flowers. He makes sure that there (ア) flowers all the year round, because our garden, like a dozen others near here, (イ) open to the public.

Even though we have all kinds of blossoms in our garden, [4]not many people come here. Most of the visitors (ウ) old ... too old to drive. So they need some kind of public transportation. There (エ) a bus service that goes around the local villages, but it is very inconvenient. The bus stop is too far away from our garden, and the timetable doesn't give (a)(enough / for / time / visitors) to carefully look round. I think I (オ) going to ask the city transport office (b)(changes / make / some / to) that will increase our number of visitors.

Notes　**take an early retirement**「早期退職する」　**fresh air**「新鮮な空気」　**look after**「手入れをする」　**a dozen**「多くの」　**city transport office**「都市交通局」

1 ア〜オに入る適切な形の be 動詞 (am, is, are) を書きなさい。

ア. (　　　　　)　イ. (　　　　　)　ウ. (　　　　　)　エ. (　　　　　)　オ. (　　　　　)

2 指示に従って書き換えなさい。

1. 下線部 1 の in the country を問う疑問文に

2. 下線部 2 の old を new に代えて否定文に

3 下線部 3 の That が示す内容を日本語で答えなさい。

4 下線部 4 の文が示す具体的な理由を日本語で答えなさい。

5 本文の内容に合うように、空所に与えられた文字で始まる文中の単語を書きなさい。

1. Her father decided to leave the (f　　　　　　　).
2. The bus stops are located in (i　　　　　　　　　) places.
3. The bus stops are a long way (f　　　　　　　) the garden.

6 次の単語の最も強く発音する箇所を答えなさい。

1. fac・to・ry
　ア　イ　ウ

2. re・tire・ment
　ア　イ　ウ

3. trans・por・ta・tion
　ア　イ　ウ　エ

4. time・ta・ble
　ア　イ　ウ

5. care・ful・ly
　ア　イ　ウ

7 (a) (b) の語を正しく並べ替えなさい。

(a) (enough / for / time / visitors)

(b) (changes / make / some / to)

2 Conversation

A 日本文を参考にして（　）の語句を正しく並べ替えなさい。ただし文頭に来る語も小文字にしてある。

1. (any / did / have / success / you)?（うまく行きましたか）

2. I (all / at / have / idea / no).（全然わかりません）

3. He promised (and / at / look / the timetable / to) change it.
（彼は時刻表を見て変更することを約束しました）

B **A** の英文 (1) ～ (3) を、適切な空所 (a) ～ (c) に入れて会話を完成しなさい。 CD 03

W: You'll never guess where I went this morning.
M: (a) Where did you go?
W: I talked to a man in the city transport office.
M: (b)
W: Yes, I think so. (c).
M: Wow. That's amazing. His usual reply to me for five years was, "No, I can't."

C 質問に対する正しい答えを (A) (B) から選びなさい。

1. Where did the woman go today?
   (A) To a large flower garden.　　(B) To the city transport office.
2. What is the man in the office going to do?
   (A) He will say "No" again.　　(B) He will try to make a new timetable.

Grammar　be 動詞

be 動詞の現在形は「人・物は～です」、過去形は「人・物は～でした」と、主語の様子や状態を表します。be 動詞は主語に合わせて形が変わります。

1. be 動詞の形

主語		現在形	否定形・短縮形	過去形	否定形・短縮形
単数	I	am	am not	was	was not / wasn't
	You	are	are not / aren't	were	were not / weren't
	He / She / It	is	is not / isn't	was	was not / wasn't
複数	We / You / They	are	are not / aren't	were	were not / weren't

☞ be 動詞の否定形は not を be 動詞のあとにつけます。

2. 主語と be 動詞の短縮形

I am→I'm　　You are→You're　　He is→He's　　It is→It's　　They are→ They're
☞主語と短縮できるのは現在形のみで過去形はありません。

3. 疑問文

・be 動詞＋主語？
Is he Michael?（彼はマイケルですか）

・疑問詞 (Who, Whose, What, Where, When, Why, How) ＋ be 動詞？
What is this?（これは何ですか）

4. 否定文

・be 動詞＋not
She is **not** lonely anymore.（彼女はもう寂しくありません）

Unit 2 Do you trust your GPS?

1 Reading

02 CD 04

We have just come home from taking a holiday. Before we left, it took the four of us a while to agree on where to go. Our two teenage children never seem to want to agree with their parents! Eventually, though, France was the winner. We planned to drive around some villages and along the coast and look at the old-style country life. We rented a car and decided to use the GPS that came with it. It seemed like a simple device. We inputted the name of the village near to where we wanted to go, and then followed the directions of a woman with a pleasant voice.

On the first day, an hour after we should have arrived, the GPS voice told us we had reached our destination. That was unbelievable, since we should have been heading south along the coast but now we were miles inland and going north. However, we can't completely blame the GPS device. The cottage in the village is in the middle of nowhere and has a name on its gate. The name is the same as that of the cottage in the village that we were trying to find. We were in the wrong village!

Notes **a while**「しばらく」 **GPS** (= Global Positioning System)「ジーピーエス」人工衛星で現在位置を測定するシステム **come with**「〜に付いている」 **in the middle of nowhere**「何もない辺ぴな場所」

1 次の単語の意味を (a) 〜 (e) から選び、下線上にその記号を書きなさい。

1. pleasant _____
2. blame _____
3. directions _____
4. destination _____
5. cottage _____

(a) a place to which a person is going
(b) a small house in the country
(c) enjoyable and making you feel happy
(d) the information that tells you how to get somewhere
(e) to consider someone responsible for a mistake

2 次の英文が本文の内容に合っていれば T、違っていれば F を選びなさい。

1. It was easy for the family to decide where to go. T F
2. The GPS machine was very difficult to use. T F
3. The GPS voice told the driver where to go. T F

2 Conversation

A 会話を聞いて空所に単語を書きなさい。 CD 05

M: Where shall we go for our summer holiday?

W: Not Italy again. The hotel was too $_1$(   ).

M: I think so, too. Then, what $_2$(   ) Switzerland and its beautiful mountains?

W: The last time we drove around the mountains, we all got car $_3$(   ).

M: Well, France has everything —country, city, sea, and mountains.

W: Right. Since $_4$(   ) is objecting, it's done.

B 質問を聞いて空所に単語を書き、適切な答えを (A) (B) から選びなさい。 CD 06

1. What was the main form of (   ) in Switzerland for the family?
   (A) By car.   (B) By train.

2. Which country did they eventually (   ) for their next holiday?
   (A) France.   (B) Switzerland.

3 Short Talk

イラストを見ながら、空所に入る単語を語群より選び文章を完成しなさい。

having
like
off
resort
trusted

I love this hi-tech world. You can do almost anything, $_1$(   ) booking your holidays abroad without ever $_2$(   ) to leave your house. For example, I was able to find which $_3$(   ) has a lot of snow, book my hotel, and even book my skis. Then I set $_4$(   ) in my car. The journey took much longer than I had planned, however. I always $_5$(   ) my GPS, but now I'm wondering. Hey! Where am I? What am I doing on this sunny beach?

Unit 3 The History of the Village　一般動詞

Warm-up

次の日本語を参考にして、空所に与えられた文字で始まる単語を書きなさい。

年　アパート　舗装する　～ですね

1. This is a beach ... blue sky and sea, and a new high-rise (a　　　　　　　) building.
2. It's beautiful, (i　　　　　　) it? Well, today it is.
3. What will it be like if we come back here in a few more (y　　　　　　)? Will the beaches be (p　　　　　　)?

1 Reading

CD 07

Oh, look! There is a tourist coach, and a lot of people (a)(are / cameras / getting / with) out of it. I wonder (b)(the tourists / to / want / what) look at? The tour guide is a young woman and [1]she has a yellow flag. Now she is talking to the tourists and telling them about the history of the village and these old houses.

Many years ago, most of the local people ア(work) in the gold mines because they had a chance to get lucky and become rich, but the mines were very dangerous. The priest of the church イ(warn) the locals not to forget to pray and thank God for their business success. However, [2]the local workers became greedy and ウ(want) even more money. Many of those workers エ(die) in mining accidents. Then, when the gold became difficult to find, the mining business オ(stop) and the mines closed down. Look at the church's garden. You can see that [3]it is overgrown with weeds. The story goes that if the priest spends too much time cleaning the garden, the village will become unlucky again.

Notes **tourist coach**「観光バス」　**gold mine**「金鉱」　**the locals**「地元の人々」　**close down**「閉鎖する」

1 ア～オの動詞を適切な形にしなさい。

ア. (　　　　　　　)　イ. (　　　　　　　)　ウ. (　　　　　　　)

エ. (　　　　　　　)　オ. (　　　　　　　)

2 指示に従って単語を変えなさい。

1. young（名詞に）＿＿＿＿＿＿＿＿　　2. success（動詞に）＿＿＿＿＿＿＿＿
3. lucky（副詞に）＿＿＿＿＿＿＿＿　　4. dangerous（反意語に）＿＿＿＿＿＿＿＿
5. difficult（反意語に）＿＿＿＿＿＿＿＿

3 指示に従って書き換えなさい。

1. 下線部 1 の a yellow flag を問う疑問文に

＿＿＿＿＿＿＿＿＿＿＿＿＿＿＿＿＿＿＿＿＿＿＿＿＿＿＿＿＿＿

2. 下線部 2 を否定文に

＿＿＿＿＿＿＿＿＿＿＿＿＿＿＿＿＿＿＿＿＿＿＿＿＿＿＿＿＿＿

4 下線部 3 の it が示す内容を日本語で答えなさい。

＿＿＿＿＿＿＿＿＿＿＿＿＿＿＿＿＿＿＿＿＿＿＿＿＿＿＿＿＿＿

5 次の単語の下線部の発音と同じ発音の語をア～エから選びなさい。

1. mine	ア. sick	イ. hill	ウ. rich	エ. wild
2. church	ア. chef	イ. child	ウ. machine	エ. stomach
3. priest	ア. believe	イ. die	ウ. friend	エ. necktie

6 本文の内容に合うように、空所に与えられた文字で始まる文中の単語を書きなさい。

1. The tourists got to the village by (c　　　　　).
2. It seems that the tourists are interested in the village's (h　　　　　).
3. Becoming unlucky is the penalty for wasting (t　　　　　).

7 (a) (b) の語句を正しく並べ替えなさい。

(a) (are / cameras / getting / with)

＿＿＿＿＿＿＿＿＿＿＿＿＿＿＿＿＿＿＿＿＿＿＿＿＿＿＿＿＿＿

(b) (the tourists / to / want / what)

＿＿＿＿＿＿＿＿＿＿＿＿＿＿＿＿＿＿＿＿＿＿＿＿＿＿＿＿＿＿

2 Conversation

A 日本文を参考にして（　）の語句を正しく並べ替えなさい。ただし文頭に来る語も小文字にしてある。

1. I've (burned / dinner / just / tonight's).（今夜の夕食を焦がしてしまいました）

＿＿＿＿＿＿＿＿＿＿＿＿＿＿＿＿＿＿＿＿＿＿＿＿＿＿＿＿＿＿

2. (anything / bad / did / happen)?（何か悪いことが起こりましたか）

＿＿＿＿＿＿＿＿＿＿＿＿＿＿＿＿＿＿＿＿＿＿＿＿＿＿＿＿＿＿

3. Hey, (coming / from / smell / that funny / what's) the kitchen?
（おや、台所から来るあの変な臭いは何ですか）

＿＿＿＿＿＿＿＿＿＿＿＿＿＿＿＿＿＿＿＿＿＿＿＿＿＿＿＿＿＿

B **A** の英文 (1) ～ (3) を、適切な空所 (a) ～ (c) に入れて会話を完成しなさい。 CD 08

W: You believe the old stories, but I don't believe them at all.

M: You helped the priest cut the weeds in the church's garden today. (a)

W: No, of course not.

M: (b)

W: Oh no! (c)

M: Now do you believe them?

C 質問に対する正しい答えを (A) (B) から選びなさい。

1. Which of these is true?
   (A) The man believes the old stories. (B) The man is preparing dinner.

2. What do you think caused the bad luck today?
   (A) Buying lunch at the supermarket. (B) Cutting the weeds in the church's garden.

Grammar 一般動詞

動作や状態を表すとき、be 動詞以外の動詞を一般動詞と言います。

1. 三単現（三人称単数現在）の場合は -s(es)

She **plays** the violin.（彼女はバイオリンを弾きます）

2. 一般動詞を使った否定文

☞ 動詞の前に do not / don't、三単現の場合は does not / doesn't ＋動詞の原形

I **don't** like carrot.（にんじんは好きではありません）

He **doesn't** know the facts.（彼は事実を知りません）

3. 一般動詞を使った疑問文

☞ 疑問文は文頭に Do、三単現の場合は Does ＋動詞の原形？

☞ 過去形の場合は Did ＋動詞の原形？

Do you go out for lunch?（ランチに出かけますか）

Does he eat breakfast?（彼は朝食を食べますか）

Did you finish your report?（レポートを終えましたか）

4. 規則動詞の過去・過去分詞形

☞ 原形に -ed (look - looked - looked)

☞ e で終わるものは -d (arrive - arrived - arrived)

☞ 子音字＋ y で終わるものは y を i に変えて -ed (study - studied - studied)

☞ 短母音＋子音字で終わるものは子音字を重ねて -ed (plan - planned -planned)

5. 規則動詞の過去・過去分詞形 [-ed] の音

☞ 動詞の語末の音によります。

有声音→ [d]：lived [lívd]「**リ**ブド」 pulled [púld]「**プ**ルド」

無声音→ [t]：worked [wə́ːkt]「**ワ**ークト」 looked [lúkt]「**ル**ックト」

[t][d] → [id]：started [stáːrti(d)]「ス**タ**ーティ（ド）」 ended [éndid]「**エ**ンディド」

Unit 4 Waiting for a Plane

1 Reading

03 CD 09

An elderly woman walked slowly into the airport waiting lounge heading for gate number seventeen. "There are a lot of people here." She said to herself, but loud enough for others to hear. She found a space for one person in the middle of the bench seats.

"Do you mind if I sit here?" she said to the young man whose bags had spread in front of his seat. He quickly pulled his bags into one pile and squeezed them with his legs so that they used a smaller space. "No, go ahead," the young man said. "This is the gate for the London flight, isn't it?" she asked. "Yes it is, but let's check your boarding pass just to make sure. Look. Here is the flight number, and it says gate number 17, and this is your seat number, 43 C. So you are in an aisle seat at the back of the plane, and boarding starts in half an hour.

She thanked him, then asked, "Are you going to London for the summer?" "Yes," the young man said. "I've just finished a course in Paris about Hotel Catering. It was hard work but I learnt a lot, and now I have to look for a job."

Notes **waiting lounge**「待合室」 **go ahead**「どうぞ」 **boarding pass**「搭乗券」 **aisle seat**「通路側の席」

1 次の単語の意味を (a) ～ (e) から選び、下線上にその記号を書きなさい。

1. spread _____
2. pile _____
3. squeeze _____
4. row _____
5. boarding _____

(a) a line of seats
(b) the act of getting on a plane
(c) things put one on top of another
(d) to place things over a large area
(e) to press together the sides of something

2 次の英文が本文の内容に合っていれば T、違っていれば F を選びなさい。

1. The woman sat down next to a young man in the airport waiting lounge. T F
2. The man made sure that she was at the right gate. T F
3. She has a window seat near the centre of the plane. T F

2 Conversation

A 会話を聞いて空所に単語を書きなさい。 CD 10

M: I wonder why our plane isn't boarding yet. Is something $_1$( ) with it?

W: No. I overheard someone say that a VIP is $_2$( ) this flight.

M: Oh, really? I wonder who the Very Important Person is.

W: He is always on TV, and he has long white $_3$( ).

M: Let me see, it's, er ... Ah, I think it's something like Ford, er ... Sandyford, maybe.

W: Right. I've $_4$( ) it. It's Oxford, Dave Oxford. I saw his program on TV.

B 質問を聞いて空所に単語を書き、適切な答えを (A) (B) から選びなさい。 CD 11

1. Why was the plane ( )?
   (A) The VIP was getting on it.
   (B) There were many planes waiting to board and take off.

2. Where had the woman got her ( ) about the VIP?
   (A) She heard someone talking about him.
   (B) She saw a TV programme about him.

3 Short Talk

イラストを見ながら、空所に入る単語を語群より選び文章を完成しなさい。

close
cool
crowded
interesting
winter

I love this airport. It's warm in $_1$( ) and $_2$( ) in summer. It's not $_3$( ) today, but usually there are all kinds of $_4$( ) people to see and even talk to. That little girl seems to love the airport, too, because the plane is so $_5$( ) that she can talk to it.

Unit 5 Where are my socks? 代名詞

Warm-up

次の日本語を参考にして、空所に与えられた文字で始まる単語を書きなさい。

暑さ　外に　許す　つぶす

1. I don't know his name because he isn't (a　　　　) to talk to people.
2. How can he stand (o　　　　) the castle all day?
3. How does he (k　　　　) the time on a cold winter day?
4. Does the summer (h　　　　) make him feel tired?

1 Reading

CD 12

My husband and I are having (ア) daily conversation. As always, he's asking me where his socks are. My reply is always the same, too. I say in a loud voice that [1]they are on the chair, in the corner, next to the TV. [2]He grumbles and mutters to himself, and then says that (イ) has found them, but one sock is grey and the other is blue. What should he do? At this point, he really wants (ウ) to look for (エ), but still [3]I am playing tennis with him, so to speak.

I say to (オ). "Why don't you look in the laundry basket? They are probably there." And as if we live in a magical world, he suddenly says, "Ah, here they are ... a blue one and a grey one." Still confused about how his socks have travelled [4]there, he now wonders whether he should wear one clean sock and one dirty one. [5]It seems as if a child were getting (a)(and / old / to / talking) himself, but look (b)(a bit / at / having / him) of fun on his one-man stage.

Notes　**as always**「いつものように」　**so to speak**「いわば」　**laundry basket**「洗濯物を入れるかご」　**one-man stage**「独り舞台」

1 ア～オに入る代名詞（me, our, he, him, them）を書きなさい。

ア. (　　　　)　イ. (　　　　)　ウ. (　　　　)　エ. (　　　　)　オ. (　　　　)

2 下線部 1 (they), 下線部 4 (there) が示す具体的な内容を日本語で答えなさい。

they: ____________________　　　　there: ____________________

3 指示に従って書き換えなさい。

1. 下線部 2 を過去形の文に

2. 下線部 3 の tennis を問う疑問文に

4 下線部 5 の It の用法と同じものを選びなさい。

(a) It is about 9:00 a.m.
(b) It looks like a big typhoon is coming soon.
(c) It is today that he is going there.

5 本文の内容に合うように、空所に与えられた文字で始まる文中の単語を書きなさい。

1. Their (c　　　　　　　　) never changes from day to day.
2. His wife always tells him where his socks are in a loud (v　　　　　　).
3. She thinks that her husband enjoys his one-man (s　　　　　　　).

6 次の単語の下線部の発音と同じ発音の語をア～エから選びなさい。

1. daily	ア. bargain	イ. curtain	ウ. email	エ. mountain
2. reply	ア. baby	イ. bicycle	ウ. stay	エ. type
3. loud	ア. double	イ. group	ウ. house	エ. soup

7 (a) (b) の語句を正しく並べ替えなさい。

(a) (and / old / to / talking)

(b) (a bit / at / having / him)

2 Conversation

A 日本文を参考にして（　）の単語を正しく並べ替えなさい。

1. Then, (come / did / here / why / you)?（それでは、どうしてここに来たのですか）

2. Hey, (a / answer / good / that's).（まあ、いい返事ですね）

3. Well, (are / old / getting / you).（ええ、あなたは年を取っているのです）

B **A** の英文 (1) ～ (3) を、適切な空所 (a) ～ (c) に入れて会話を完成しなさい。 CD 13

M: I can't remember why I came here.
W: (a) That's why.
M: No, I can't agree. I think it's because I am multi-tasking, and I am just busy.
W: I see. (b)
M: Maybe I just wanted to see your lovely face.
W: (c) So, do you think I still look young?

C 質問に対する正しい答えを (A) (B) から選びなさい。

1. What is the man's problem?
   (A) He can't remember his age.　　(B) He is becoming forgetful.

2. Why does he say he came to this room?
   (A) He looked young.　　(B) He wanted to see the woman's face.

Grammar　代名詞

代名詞の種類

1. 人称代名詞：we, my, him, her, mine, yourself など

☞ 話し手や聞き手、すでに前に出た名詞を言い換えるときに使います。

I saw **my** classmates. **They** were going to have a football match.
(クラスメイトに会いました。彼らはサッカーの試合をしに行くところでした)

I am Catherine. Please call **me** Kate.（私はキャサリンです。ケイトと呼んでください）

My favourite colour is blue. What is **yours**?
(私の好きな色はブルーです。あなたの好きな色は何ですか)

2. 指示代名詞：it, this, that, these, those など

☞ 前の語句や文を受けます。

I was going to use my **computer**, but **it** was out of order.
(私はコンピュータを使おうとしましたが、それは故障していました)

Paul has a new job. I didn't know **that**.
(ポールは新しい仕事をします。私はそのことを知りませんでした)

代名詞 It の用法

1. 天候・日付・時間・距離

It's a hot day today.（今日は暑いです）
It's 23 May today.（今日は 5 月 23 日です）
It's 7 a.m. now.（今、午前 7 時です）
It's about 100 metres.（約 100 メートルです）

2. 形式主語

It is necessary **to lose weight**.（体重を減らすことが必要です）
It is certain **that he will succeed in business**.（彼はきっと仕事で成功します）

Unit 6 Are you all right?

1 Reading

04 CD 14

Every Wednesday is Brenda's shopping day. She leaves work half an hour earlier than usual and goes to the supermarket in High Street, where she always buys a lot of stuff. Today, she came out of the store carrying two large bags that were filled with groceries. Brenda is a great person. Her head is always full of ideas, like what to cook for the party at the weekend or where to go for a summer holiday. She is a non-stop multi-tasker. On Wednesday, she was lost in thought about what to make for dinner and wasn't concentrating on where she was walking.

Unfortunately, she tripped on the uneven pavement and fell down heavily — and her shopping went all over the road. A young man and woman who were walking nearby ran around collecting her stuff for her. A middle-aged woman, who was probably an off-duty nurse, very professionally checked Brenda for injuries and suggested that Brenda should go to hospital. A taxi that happened to be across the road came over, and the driver said he would take her to the Royal Anne Hospital for free.

Notes **multi-tasker**「多くのことを同時にできる人」 **be lost in thought**「思いにふける」 **trip**「つまずく」 **off-duty**「非番の」

1 次の単語の意味を (a) ～ (e) から選び、下線上にその記号を書きなさい。

1. concentrate _____
2. uneven _____
3. nearby _____
4. suggest _____
5. free _____

(a) not costing any money
(b) not far away
(c) not flat or smooth
(d) to focus your attention on the thing
(e) to recommend something

2 次の英文が本文の内容に合っていれば T、違っていれば F を選びなさい。

1. She goes shopping on a weekday. T F
2. She tripped and fell because she was thinking about today's dinner. T F
3. People Brenda knew came to help her. T F

2 Conversation

A 会話を聞いて空所に単語を書きなさい。 CD 15

W: Something very odd happened today. A woman walked into the hospital this morning. I guess she was in her $_1$(　　　　　　　). She was carrying two shopping bags.

M: So, what was strange about that?

W: When the receptionist asked her for her name and address, the woman couldn't remember where she $_2$(　　　　　　　). When I looked at her closely, I saw that she had a cut on her knee. Oh, and she had a bruise on her $_3$(　　　　　　　). I asked her, "Did you fall down?" but she didn't answer.

M: Did you $_4$(　　　　　　　) the police?

W: Yes, we did, but the woman wasn't able to answer their questions.

B 質問を聞いて空所に単語を書き、適切な答えを (A) (B) から選びなさい。 CD 16

1. What did the woman (　　　　　　　) like?
   (A) She was middle-aged and carrying two shopping bags.
   (B) She was very young and quite beautiful.

2. Did she have any (　　　　　　　)?
   (A) She couldn't hear what the receptionist said.
   (B) She had a cut on her knee.

3 Short Talk

イラストを見ながら、空所に入る単語を語群より選び文章を完成しなさい。

above
designed
playing
shopping
why

Harry stands out in a crowd—literally. That's because he towers $_1$(　　　　　　　) almost everyone else. He told me that $_2$(　　　　　　　) sports for tall boys in school—like basketball—wasn't much fun because it was too easy for him. I don't know $_3$(　　　　　　　) he came to Japan. The houses here are $_4$(　　　　　　　) for much shorter people, and he knows that $_5$(　　　　　　　) for clothes will always be very difficult. I don't envy him at all. In fact, I pity him.

Unit 7 Checking in at a Hotel 数詞

Warm-up

次の日本語を参考にして、空所に与えられた文字で始まる単語を書きなさい。

入り口　建物　言う　着く

1. A taxi has just (a　　　　　　) at the hotel's (e　　　　　　).
2. A porter is (t　　　　　　) the driver where to stop.
3. I wonder what the main (b　　　　　　) looks like.

1 Reading

CD 17

Our tour bus arrived at the hotel in Honolulu on schedule. The driver and the hotel staff unloaded our luggage and put [1]it in the lobby. "Hello. I am Peter Bright from Luxury Travels," I said to the reception staff. The hotel manager cut me off and said, "Just bear with me for a couple of minutes, and I can finish with this previous group."

"Now, I'm sorry to have kept you waiting. How many guests are there in your group, sir?" the manager asked. [2]I showed him my booking details and said, "Twenty-eight. So I need (ア) singles and a dozen twin rooms. We are staying for (イ) nights." [3]He wanted my office telephone number. I said, "Sure, it's [4]041-336-2800." The man smiled and thanked me, and gave me a handful of keys. He said they were the keys for the whole group, but he was sorry that he couldn't put us all together. Half will be on the (ウ) floor and the rest on the (エ) floor. In a loud and pleasant voice, I (a)(asked / check / my group / to) if the TV, phone, and air conditioner were all working, and if hot water actually (b)(of / out / came / the tap).

Notes **Honolulu**「ホノルル」アメリカ合衆国ハワイ州の州都　**bear with me**「少しお待ちください」
a handful of「一握りの」　**put ... all together**「～をまとめる」

1 ア～エに入る数字の綴りを書きなさい。

ア．シングル４つ：(　　　　　　) singles　　イ．３泊：(　　　　　　) nights

ウ．２階［アメリカ英語］：the (　　　　　　) floor

エ．３階［アメリカ英語］：the (　　　　　　) floor

2 下線部 1 の it が示す内容を日本語で答えなさい。

3 次の単語の下線部の発音と同じ発音の語をア～エから選びなさい。

1. arrived　　ア. asked　イ. moved　ウ. started　エ. visited
2. unloaded　　ア. finished　イ. laughed　ウ. stayed　エ. wanted
3. thanked　　ア. hoped　イ. raised　ウ. showed　エ. travelled

4 指示に従って書き換えなさい。

1. 下線部 2 を否定文に

2. 下線部 3 の my office telephone number を問う疑問文に

5 下線部 4 の電話番号の読み方を書きなさい。

6 本文の内容に合うように、空所に与えられた文字で始まる文中の単語を書きなさい。

1. The guests don't have to handle their (l　　　　　) by themselves.
2. The hotel staff told me to wait for 2 or 3 (m　　　　　) at the front desk.
3. He needs sixteen (r　　　　　) for 3 nights.

7 (a) (b) の語句を正しく並べ替えなさい。

(a) (asked / check / my group / to)

(b) (of / out / came / the tap)

2 Conversation

A 日本文を参考にして（　）の語句を正しく並べ替えなさい。ただし文頭に来る語も小文字にしてある。

1. They're (both / in / place / same / the).（どちらも同じ場所です）

2. You need to (at / hand / in / meal ticket / your) the entrance.
（入り口で食券を提出する必要があります）

3. (all / be / right / that / would)?（それで、よろしいでしょうか）

B **A** の英文 (1) ～ (3) を、適切な空所 (a) ～ (c) に入れて会話を完成しなさい。 CD 18

M: What time is breakfast?

W: It is from 7:00 to 10:00. (a)

M: Where are the breakfast and dinner rooms?

W: (b) In the main restaurant, at the end of this corridor. I would like your group to meet on time and to sit together at meal times. (c)

M: Yes, that's fine.

W: Thank you very much. I hope you enjoy your stay.

C 質問に対する正しい答えを (A) (B) から選びなさい。

1. What time does breakfast finish?
   (A) 7:00.　　(B) 10:00.

2. What does the hotel want the group to do?
   (A) To keep together in the restaurant.　　(B) To sit separately.

Grammar　数詞

1. 名詞の前

This high-rise building has sixty **floors**.（この高層ビルは 60 階建てです）

2. 漠然と多数

This library has hundreds of hobby books.（この図書館は何百冊もの趣味の本があります）

☞ hundreds of（何百もの～）　thousands of（何千もの～）　tens of thousands of（何万もの～）

3. 数の読み方

101 → a / one hundred (and) one

100,000,000,000

↓ thousand（千）

↓ million（100 万）

↓ billion（10 億）

4. 少数の読み方

40.234 → forty point two three four

5. 金額の読み方

97 ドル 85 セント → ninety-seven (dollars) eighty-five (cents)

29,600 円 → twenty-nine thousand (and) six hundred yen

6. 年号日付の読み方

1994 年 → nineteen ninety-four / nineteen hundred ninety-four

2020 年 → twenty-twenty / two thousand and twenty

7 月 3 日 → July the third [3rd], July 3 ＜米式は月・日の順＞

the third [3rd] of July, 3 July ＜英式は日・月の順＞

7. 電話番号の読み方

321- 6054 → three two one six oh [zero] five four

☞ 0 は [oh] または [zero] と読み、ハイフンは読みません。

Unit 8 Tour Schedule

1 Reading

05 19

I've just looked at the weather forecast for tomorrow. It says that we will have some nice, dry weather until lunchtime, but in the afternoon it might rain. So that means you should not forget to take your umbrellas with you. Have any of you been here before? No? Well, that's great, because it means you are all in for a real treat. Now then, here's what we are scheduled to do in the morning. We'll walk down the hill, and then go across the river on that bridge. You can see it from here. It's the one with all the little shops on it. After that we'll turn right, and the road leads into the main tourist area.

As I said, there's a chance of rain tomorrow, but the churches, museums, and shops are all close together, so you shouldn't get too wet. The place will be packed with tourists, so please don't be late for your meeting points. If you do become separated from your group, call me at my mobile number. Make sure to charge your phones before you go to bed tonight, and of course, don't forget your contact numbers and a map of the hotel.

Notes **weather forecast**「天気予報」 **be all in for a real treat**「大いに楽しめる」 **lead into**「～に通じる」 **chance of rain**「雨が降る可能性」 **meeting point**「集合場所」 **make sure**「必ず～する」

1 次の単語の意味を (a) ～ (e) から選び、下線上にその記号を書きなさい。

1. dry _____
2. area _____
3. charge _____
4. separate _____
5. contact _____

(a) section; part
(b) having no rain
(c) a way of getting in touch with others
(d) to put electricity into a battery
(e) to stop being a part of

2 次の英文が本文の内容に合っていれば T、違っていれば F を選びなさい。

1. The best weather will be in the morning. T F
2. The weather will change in the afternoon. T F
3. It will be hot tomorrow, so they should take a hat. T F

2 Conversation

A 会話を聞いて空所に単語を書きなさい。 CD 20

W: When we go into the church, I'd like you to $_{1}$(   ) a couple of things.
M: No problem. What are they?
W: You have to $_{2}$(   ) off your hats at the entrance.
M: Anything else?
W: You can take photos in the church, but $_{3}$(   ) use a flash.
M: Is there an entry $_{4}$(   )?
W: No, not here. If you want, you can put some money into the collection box.

B 質問を聞いて空所に単語を書き、適切な答えを (A) (B) から選びなさい。 CD 21

1. What aren't they (   ) to do in this church?
   (A) Take photos. (B) Wear a hat.

2. What can they (   ) to do?
   (A) Put money in the collection box. (B) Pay the entry fee.

3 Short Talk

イラストを見ながら、空所に入る単語を語群より選び文章を完成しなさい。

back between built design what

The bus is stopping. Everyone out, please. Now listen carefully to $_{1}$(   ) the guide is telling us. She says the two churches were both $_{2}$(   ) in the 13th century. They are similar in $_{3}$(   ), but they are for different religions. There is a souvenir shop $_{4}$(   ) the churches. Be $_{5}$(   ) here at the bus in 40 minutes. Don't be late!

Unit 9 House for Sale　前置詞・接続詞

Warm-up

次の日本語を参考にして、空所に与えられた文字で始まる単語を書きなさい。

ライフスタイル　家具　見る　使う

1. When you get married, what kind of (l　　　　　　) do you expect to live?
2. Some couples will (s　　　　　　) money on big things like (f　　　　　　) and a nice apartment.
3. In this photo, a young couple are (l　　　　　　) at the information board.

1 Reading

CD 22

Did I mention that we are selling our house? It's only been (ア) the market (イ) a month, so not many people know about it yet. Ted and I think it is a perfect house, (ウ) our asking price is a bit high because we put a lot of work into the house and the garden. For example, the kitchen has been completely remodeled, so [1]<u>it</u> is perfect. And we spent a fortune making the front garage and gate look just right.

[2]<u>Last weekend a young couple came to look at the house.</u> The wife fell in love with it, but the price is a bit steep. Do you remember that our house is on a hill? On one side, the house overlooks the city, and on the other side is a view of hills (エ) trees. A couple of years ago we had the builder put in a floor-to-ceiling window (オ) the living room, so the view has become even better, especially (カ) the seasons change. [3]<u>Ted doesn't really want to leave.</u> You know how men are! But he has got a promotion and the daily (a)(be / commute / too / will) far, so we are (b)(for / looking / similar / something) in North Wales.

Notes　**spend a fortune**「大金を費やす」　**fall in love with**「～を気に入る」　**put in**「～を取り付ける」
floor-to-ceiling window「床から天井まである窓」

1 ア～オに接続詞 (and, but, when)、または前置詞 (for, in, on) を入れなさい。

ア. (　　　　)　イ. (　　　　)　ウ. (　　　　)　エ. (　　　　)　オ. (　　　　)　カ. (　　　　)

2 指示に従って単語を変えなさい。

1. high（名詞に） ________________　　2. replace（名詞に） ________________

3. remember（名詞に） ________________　　4. change（形容詞に） ________________

5. promotion（動詞に） ________________

3 下線部 1 の it が示す内容を日本語で答えなさい。

____

4 指示に従って書き換えなさい。

1. 下線部 2 の last weekend を next weekend にして未来形の文に

____

2. 下線部 3 を肯定文に

____

5 本文の内容に合うように、空所に与えられた文字で始まる文中の単語を書きなさい。

1. The house is for sale, but only a few (p　　　　　　) have come to look at it.
2. The view from the window is better when the (s　　　　　　) turn.
3. Ted has to move because of his (p　　　　　　　　).

6 次の単語の最も強く発音する箇所を答えなさい。

1. ex·am·ple
　ア　イ　ウ

2. com·plete·ly
　ア　イ　ウ

3. re·mem·ber
　ア　イ　ウ

4. es·pe·cial·ly
　ア　イ　ウ　エ

5. com·mute
　ア　イ

7 (a) (b) の語を正しく並べ替えなさい。

(a) (be / commute / too / will)

____

(b) (for / looking / similar / something)

____

2 Conversation

A 日本文を参考にして（　）の語を正しく並べ替えなさい。ただし文頭に来る語も小文字にしてある。

1. (are / around / from / here / they)?（彼らはこのあたりの出身ですか）

____

2. Yes, I (means / see / she / what).（はい、彼女が言いたいことはわかります）

____

3. Well, they won't (about / any / getting / have / worries) a housing loan, then, will they?
（ええと、じゃあ彼らは住宅ローンを組むことを心配する必要はありませんね）

____

B **A** の英文 (1) ～ (3) を、適切な空所 (a) ～ (c) に入れて会話を完成しなさい。 CD 23

W: The estate agent said that a young couple are interested in buying our house.

M: (a)

W: Yes. The man works in a local bank, and the woman is a teacher.

M: (b)

W: The only problem is that she says she might be lonely in the country.

M: (c).

C 質問に対する正しい答えを (A) (B) から選びなさい。

1. Who might buy the house?
   (A) A local banker and his wife. (B) An older couple from abroad.

2. What problem does the possible new owner have about the house?
   (A) She is worried they won't be able to get a housing loan.
   (B) She thinks the house might be a little lonely.

Grammar 前置詞・接続詞

前置詞

☞名詞・代名詞の前に置き、時・場所・理由・方法などを表します。

Mason is speaking for half an hour.（メイソンは 30 分間話しています）

We arrived at the office in the morning.（私たちは午前中にオフィスに着きました）

Olivia went to school either by bicycle or on foot.（オリビアは自転車か徒歩で通学しました）

接続詞

☞語・句・文を接続します。

1. 等位接続詞：語・句・文を対等に結ぶ（and, but, for, nor, or）

Owen drank wine and beer for dinner.（オーウェンは夕食でワインとビールを飲みました）

Grace wanted to buy a house, but she could not afford it.
（グレースは家を買いたいと思いましたが、その余裕はありませんでした）

2. 従位接続詞：名詞節を導く (if, that, whether)、副詞節を導く (although, as, because, if, since, until, when, while)

I don't know if Stella will buy a condo. ＜名詞節＞
（ステラがマンションを買うのかどうかわかりません）

If he has a job interview, he will get the job. ＜副詞節＞
（もし面接を受ければ、彼はその仕事に就けるでしょう）

Unit 10 The City

1 Reading

06 CD 24

I was really excited. I hadn't seen my friend Debbie since she had got married, and I was looking forward to seeing her new apartment in the city. Debbie had said she had to work until 3:00 pm, so I decided to drive into the city early, leave the car somewhere, and then walk around and do some shopping. The city centre with its high-rise buildings was newer and bigger than I had thought it would be.

The shopping malls were a great surprise. They offered as much shopping variety as my own city. The prices were pretty good, too, so I was able to pick up some bargain souvenirs for my family. I wanted to buy some cargo pants, and in a sports wear shop, I found just what I had wanted, but unfortunately there was nothing that fit me. I was ready to walk out and go somewhere else, but the young assistant didn't give up. He asked me to sit down and wait while he checked the goods on his computer.

Eventually, his worried face was replaced with a big smile, and he asked me to come back tomorrow afternoon, because by then he would have a large selection of sizes and colours of the style I wanted. Wow! Perth really was a city with a warm heart.

Notes **high-rise building**「高層ビル」 **pick up**「～を買う」 **cargo pants**「カーゴパンツ」ポケットのある厚手の木綿製ズボン **Perth**「パース」西オーストラリア州の州都

1 次の単語の意味を (a) ～ (e) から選び、下線上にその記号を書きなさい。

1. decide _____
2. variety _____
3. assistant _____
4. fit _____
5. replace _____

(a) a large collection of different things
(b) a person whose job is to help customers
(c) to be the right size and shape
(d) to change or exchange one thing for another
(e) to make a choice about something

2 次の英文が本文の内容に合っていれば T、違っていれば F を選びなさい。

1. Debbie was about to get married and move to a new city. T F
2. Debbie couldn't get off work until mid-afternoon. T F
3. In the city centre, everything was very expensive. T F

2 Conversation

A 会話を聞いて空所に単語を書きなさい。 CD 25

M: Jeans with pictures on the back pockets for young kids? No. I'm sorry but we don't carry anything like $_{1}$(   ).

W: Do you know where I can try to $_{2}$(   ) some?

M: There's a jeans shop in Newtown, but the internet is your best $_{3}$(   ).

W: Right. Thanks a lot. I'll $_{4}$(   ) it a try when I get back home.

M: Best of luck.

W: Cheers.

B 質問を聞いて空所に単語を書き、適切な答えを (A) (B) から選びなさい。 CD 26

1. What did the woman (   ) about kids' jeans?
   (A) The style she wanted was not available in the man's shop.
   (B) The style she wanted was in stock at the man's shop.

2. Which way of (   ) for the jeans sounds better?
   (A) Call in and ask at several shops.   (B) Looking on the internet.

3 Short Talk

イラストを見ながら、空所に入る単語を語群より選び文章を完成しなさい。

close
collection
different
most
why

We came here because people told me it was an exciting city. The high-rise buildings are standing $_{1}$(   ) together with little space between them. I wonder $_{2}$(   ) they did that? The place that I like $_{3}$(   ) is outside the city centre. It is a $_{4}$(   ) of about five-storey-high office buildings, and they are all of $_{5}$(   ) colours and shapes, with no coordination among them. That's why, to me, the place looks so attractive.

Unit 11 Our Company　助動詞・完了形

Warm-up

次の日本語を参考にして、空所に与えられた文字で始まる単語を書きなさい。

髪　真ん中　セーター　メガネ

1. The boy wearing (g　　　　) seems to be the most serious of the group.
2. The girl in the (m　　　　) is womanly and wearing a striped (s　　　　).
3. The third one, the girl looking behind her, has long blonde (h　　　　).

1 Reading

CD 27

Hi, I'm Betty, and you [ア](must / should) be Thomas. I've been ①(tell) to show you around our company. I [イ](can / could) do that OK for now, but after lunch I am busy, so you [ウ](will / would) be on your own. Is [1]<u>that</u> all right with you? I think he said yes, but [2]<u>I was too busy to ask him again</u>.

Now, in our company we've ②(get) a large office. [3]<u>We do two things here.</u> One is to keep track of all the truck parts that come in and go out. The other is to try to design better parts that we can make more cheaply. I'm sure you have ③(see) all those little trucks running around delivering things for shops and construction companies. Well, we make most of the clips and joints that connect the engine, steering, brakes, etc. Now then, [(a)](if / to / want / work / you) here, [(b)](begin / in / you / would) the factory. It is a noisy place and the pay is not so good, but you can work your way up the ladder year by year.

Notes　**show ... around**「～を案内する」　**keep track of**「～を把握する」　**work one's way up the ladder**「独力で出世する」　**year by year**「年を追うごとに」

1 ア～ウの適切な助動詞を選びなさい。

ア. (　　　　)　イ. (　　　　)　ウ. (　　　　)

2 ①～③の動詞を現在完了形にするため適切な形にしなさい。

① (　　　　　　　)　② (　　　　　　　)　③ (　　　　　　　)

3 下線部 1 の that が示す内容を日本語で答えなさい。

4 指示に従って書き換えなさい。

1. 下線部 2 を so ... that ～構文に
2. 下線部 3 の two things を問う疑問文に

5 指示に従って単語を変えなさい。

1. large（反意語に）
2. deliver（名詞に）
3. construction（動詞に）
4. connect（名詞に）
5. noisy（反意語に）

6 次の単語の下線部の発音と同じ発音の語をア～エから選びなさい。

1. design	ア．positive	イ．signature	ウ．site	エ．tension
2. clips	ア．roads	イ．shoes	ウ．socks	エ．phones
3. ladder	ア．casual	イ．change	ウ．take	エ．want

7 本文の内容に合うように、空所に与えられた文字で始まる文中の単語を書きなさい。

1. Thomas has come to see this (c　　　　　　).
2. (B　　　　　　) has a little free time in the morning.
3. In this company, it seems that new workers (b　　　　　　) at the bottom.

8 (a) (b) の語を正しく並べ替えなさい。

(a) (if / to / want / work / you)

(b) (begin / in / you / would)

2 Conversation

A 日本文を参考にして（　）の語句を正しく並べ替えなさい。ただし文頭に来る語も小文字にしてある。

1. The boy (interviewed / morning / this / you).（今朝あなたが面接した若者）
2. (a chance / give / him / let's) and take him on.（彼にチャンスを与え、雇いましょう）
3. Well, my (first / good / impression / that / wasn't).
（そうね、私の第一印象はそれほど良くありませんでした）

B **A** の英文 (1) ～ (3) を、適切な空所 (a) ～ (c) に入れて会話を完成しなさい。 CD 28

M: Well, what did you think about him?
W: Who's that?
M: (a)
W: (b) He didn't speak much. But when he relaxed, he was an interesting young man.
M: So what do you recommend that we do?
W: (c)

C 質問に対する正しい答えを (A) (B) から選びなさい。

1. What impression did the boy make on the woman?
   (A) He is an outspoken lad with strong opinions.
   (B) He was too quiet and shy at first.

2. What is going to happen to him?
   (A) He will be employed.
   (B) He will have to look around for another job.

Grammar 助動詞・完了形

助動詞

1. 助動詞は動詞に意味を追加＜助動詞＋動詞の原形＞

- **will**：～だろう（未来）、～するつもりだ（意志） < 過去形は **would**>
- **can**：～できる（可能）、～してもよい（許可） < 過去形は **could**>
- **may**：～してもよい（許可）、～かもしれない（推量） < 過去形は **might**>
- **should**：～すべきだ（義務）、～のはずだ（推量）
- **must**：～しなければならない（義務）、～に違いない（推量）

You should enjoy listening to music.（あなたは音楽を聴くことを楽しむべきです）
She must go to the office.（彼女はオフィスに行かなければなりません）

2. 否定文 ＜助動詞＋ not ＞

Grace can't [can not] write the report.（グレースは報告書を書くことができません）

3. 疑問文＜助動詞＋主語＋動詞の原形～？＞

Can you show me around the company?（会社を案内してくれますか）
☞ Can you ～?, Could you ～? は「～してくれますか」と依頼を表します。

完了形

1. 現在完了形：現在までの完了・経験・継続 ＜ have / has ＋過去分詞＞

Sandra has just got to the headquarters.（サンドラは本社にちょうど着いたところです）
I have been to Norway before.（以前ノルウェーに行ったことがあります）
John has known the customer for 20 years.（ジョンはその顧客と 20 年来の知り合いです）

2. 過去完了形：過去のある時点までの完了・経験・継続 ＜ had ＋過去分詞＞

When Beth arrived at the office, the meeting had already started.
（ベスがオフィスに着いたとき、ミーティングはすでに始まっていました）

3. 未来完了形：未来のある時点における完了・経験・継続 ＜ will ＋ have ＋過去分詞＞

Brian will have finished the assignment by next Friday.
（ブライアンは来週の金曜日までにその課題を終えているでしょう）

Unit 12 At the Hospital

1 Reading

07 CD 29

A woman walked into the hospital this morning. She was on the short side, and I guessed she was in her 40s. Her clothes were smart, but not gaudy. I thought she might be a secretary from an office. She was carrying two shopping bags, but the handle of one of them was broken. The bags were full of her shopping, so I guess she was on her way home from the market when something happened.

The receptionist asked her for her name and address, but the woman couldn't remember where she lived. Later the police came and said they had examined the accident site but that they had found nothing unusual. It seems that she had somehow fallen down all by herself. When I looked at her more closely, I saw that she had a cut on her knee, and her hands were dirty. She also had broken the heel of one shoe. Oh, and she had a bruise on her forehead. We still didn't know anything about her, so we sent Bob, that new man at reception, to the local supermarket. Her credit card showed that she worked locally and lived by herself, so the doctor decided to keep her in overnight. He was going to have another look at her in the morning.

Notes **on the short side**「小柄な人で」 **on one's way home**「帰宅途中に」 **accident site**「事故現場」 **all by oneself**「自分だけで」

1 次の単語の意味を (a) ～ (e) から選び、下線上にその記号を書きなさい。

1. smart _____	(a) a dark and painful area on your skin caused by a bump
2. gaudy _____	(b) a part of something that you hold with your hand
3. handle _____	(c) stylish and fashionable
4. examine _____	(d) to look at something closely and carefully
5. bruise _____	(e) too bright and over-decorated

2 次の英文が本文の内容に合っていれば T、違っていれば F を選びなさい。

1. Somebody had been chasing the woman when she fell down. T F
2. Probably, the heel of her shoe broke when she fell. T F
3. She had cash but didn't have a credit card. T F

2 Conversation

A 会話を聞いて空所に単語を書きなさい。 CD 30

M: It seems like an unlikely story.

W: It $_1$(　　　　　　) sound that way, but it is true.

M: You said you bought two bags of groceries, ran out of the store like a $_2$(　　　　　　), and then fell down.

W: Why don't you check my bags and $_3$(　　　　　　)?

M: I've done that, and everything is in $_4$(　　　　　　). But why did you run?

W: My bus was coming.

B 質問を聞いて空所に単語を書き、適切な答えを (A) (B) から選びなさい。 CD 31

1. What kind of person did the man (　　　　　　) the woman was?
   (A) A thief in a hurry.　　(B) A woman telling an unlikely story.

2. What did the man (　　　　　　)?
   (A) The bus schedule.　　(B) The woman's bag and receipt.

3 Short Talk

イラストを見ながら、空所に入る単語を語群より選び文章を完成しなさい。

balance
coming
left
over
run

She told me she was late. She finished her shopping in a hurry, looked at her watch, and $_1$(　　　　　　) the supermarket. She said she looked $_2$(　　　　　　) her shoulder and saw her bus $_3$(　　　　　　) along the road. She began to $_4$(　　　　　　) to the bus stop, but with all her shopping and her new high heels, she lost her $_5$(　　　　　　), broke her shoe, and woke up in hospital.

Unit 13 Packing Your Bags 関係代名詞・命令文

Warm-up

次の日本語を参考にして、空所に与えられた文字で始まる単語を書きなさい。

スマートに　荷物　借りる　計画する

1. One important thing to think about when you (p) a holiday is your (l).
2. I want to look (s) when I go out for dinner.
3. If you are going skiing, you could travel light and (r) skis and other equipment when you get there.

1 Reading

CD 32

"It has never happened to me, so I don't worry about it." That's [ア](what / which) the man always says, but I wonder when his luck will run out. Have you ever seen a passenger at the airport surrounded by security staff [イ](who / whom) is having his luggage examined in detail? You see, [1]it does happen, and one day it might happen to you — unless you listen. So here's some advice about packing [ウ](that / whose) you should keep in mind when you go abroad.

First of all, [2]don't fill your suitcase. [3]Leave one third of it empty, because you are probably going to buy some souvenirs to bring back home with you. Don't put your valuables in your suitcase. Put [4]them in your hand luggage. How many nights are you going to stay? That answer will tell you how many changes of clothes you will need. Wrap your shoes in plastic shopping bags and put them at the bottom of your suitcase. Put the light things at the top. Put your passport, tickets, and other papers in your carry-on bag. When you check in, you won't see your suitcase again until you reach your destination. So keep your papers handy. Don't [(a)](a pen / forget / take / to), and, [(b)](are / if / like / old / you) me, you'll need your reading glasses.

Notes **run out**「尽きる」 **first of all**「まず第一に」 **hand luggage**「手荷物」 **changes of clothes**「着替えの服」 **keep ... handy**「～を手元に用意する」 **reading glasses**「老眼鏡」

1 ア～ウの関係代名詞で適切なものを選びなさい。

ア. (　　　　　)　イ. (　　　　　)　ウ. (　　　　　)

2 下線部 1 の it の具体的な内容を日本語で書きなさい。

3 指示に従って書き換えなさい。

1. 下線部 2 を you で始めて禁止を表す文に

2. 下線部 3 を you で始めて同じ意味の文に

4 下線部 4 の them の内容を日本語で答えなさい。

5 次の語の最も強く発音する箇所を答えなさい。

1. pas・sen・ger
ア イ ウ

2. se・cu・ri・ty
ア イ ウ エ

3. val・u・a・bles
ア イ ウ エ

4. pass・port
ア イ

5. des・ti・na・tion
ア イ ウ エ

6 本文の内容に合うように、空所に与えられた文字で始まる文中の単語を書きなさい。

1. So far, the man seems to have had a lot of luck at (a　　　　　) security.
2. For better security, don't put your expensive items in your (s　　　　　).
3. Older people should always carry their reading (g　　　　　) with them.

7 (a) (b) の語句を正しく並べ替えなさい。

(a) (a pen / forget / take / to)

(b) (are / if / like / old / you)

2 Conversation

A 日本文を参考にして (　) の語句を正しく並べ替えなさい。ただし文頭に来る語も小文字にしてある。

1. No, (all / at / like / nothing) that.（いいえ、そのようなものは全然ありません）

2. (a / good / have / trip)!（いい旅を！）

3. (by / did / this bag / pack / you) yourself?（このバッグを自分で詰めましたか）

B **A** の英文 (1) ～ (3) を、適切な空所 (a) ～ (c) に入れて会話を完成しなさい。 CD 33

M: (a)
W: Yes, I did.
M: Do you have any liquids, fresh foods, or sharp instruments in here?
W: (b)
M: Thank you. (c)
W: Thank you.

C 質問に対する正しい答えを (A) (B) から選びなさい。

1. Who put the things into the woman's bag?
(A) She did. (B) Someone else did.

2. What does she have that is not allowed?
(A) Nothing. (B) Uncooked food.

Grammar 関係代名詞・命令文

関係代名詞

☞前の名詞を説明する働き。関係代名詞＋説明文

Jennifer is **a person** who works for a travel agency. ＜主格＞
（ジェニファーは旅行代理店で働いている人です）

I have **a friend** whose mother advised me how to pack. ＜所有格＞
（母親が荷造りの仕方のアドバイスをしてくれた友だちがいます）

I saw **the photos** that Sara took. ＜目的格＞
（サラが撮った写真を見ました）

Nicole went on **a trip**, which was really relaxing. ＜非制限用法＞
（ニコルは旅行に行き、本当にくつろぎました）

先行詞	主格	所有格	目的格
人	who	whose	whom / who
物・動物	which	whose	which
人・物・動物	that	—	that

命令文

☞人に何かを命令・禁止する表現「動詞の原形＋～」

1. 肯定の命令文「～しなさい」

Have a safe trip!（行ってらっしゃい！）

2. 否定の命令文「～してはいけない」

Don't put it in the bag.（それをバッグに入れないでください）

Never put off till tomorrow what you can do today.
（今日できることを決して明日まで延ばしてはいけません）

3. 丁寧な命令文「～してください」

Please arrange the itinerary.（旅行日程を調整してください）

Enjoy your day off, **please**.（どうぞ休みを楽しんでください）

Unit 14 A Train Ticket

1 Reading

08 CD 34

Yesterday, I told Raymond, our new homestay student, about the train system here in Japan. First of all, I said, on the overhead map, find the station that you want to go to. Remember the price of the ticket. Then put that amount of money into the machine. You can put in more money than the cost of the ticket, because the machines give change. Press the button that has the correct fare, and your ticket comes out of this slot. But don't forget to collect your change. Of course, you can also buy a Pasmo card, so you don't have to bother with buying a ticket each time.

Japan's system is pretty simple, but what happens in other countries? In Germany, you have to buy a ticket from a nearby shop because the station might be and often is unmanned. Then you put your ticket into a small box that actually is a data reader. When you get off the train, you put your ticket into the gate or in another little box. Don't try to cheat the system, because quite often there are plain-clothes railway police who suddenly begin to check all the passengers' tickets. And no matter how hard you argue, the fine is a big one.

Notes **first of all**「まず第一に」 **Pasmo card**「パスモカード」交通 IC カード **data reader**「データ処理装置」 **plain-clothes railway police**「私服鉄道警察」 **no matter how**「どんなに〜であろうとも」

1 次の単語の意味を (a) 〜 (e) から選び、下線上にその記号を書きなさい。

1. change _____
2. fare _____
3. slot _____
4. unmanned _____
5. fine _____

(a) a long, thin opening
(b) an amount of money that you must pay as punishment
(c) not attended or done by a person
(d) money that you receive after paying too much
(e) the money you pay to travel on a plane, train, or bus

2 次の英文が本文の内容に合っていれば T、違っていれば F を選びなさい

1. In Japan, you have to buy your ticket at a nearby shop. T F
2. In Japan, there is no need to worry about paying too much money for a ticket. T F
3. "Honesty is the best policy" when you buy a train ticket in Germany. T F

2 Conversation

A 会話を聞いて空所に単語を書きなさい。 CD 35

M: It's easy to find our house. Which way are you $_{1}$(　　　　　　)?
W: Uphill.
M: Turn round. Drive down the hill. When you $_{2}$(　　　　　　) to the shops, go right.
W: So I turn right where Sainsbury's has a $_{3}$(　　　　　　) percent off sale?
M: That's right. Then, take the $_{4}$(　　　　　　) turn on your left.
W: Oh, I know that place. There's a classy shoe shop on the corner.

B 質問を聞いて空所に単語を書き、適切な答えを (A) (B) から選びなさい。 CD 36

1. Why most likely must the woman turn (　　　　　　)?
   (A) Because the road has ended.　　(B) Because she is going in a wrong direction.

2. What kind of (　　　　　　) does Sainsbury's have?
   (A) Everything is half price.
   (B) Things are 30 percent cheaper than the price.

3 Short Talk

イラストを見ながら、空所に入る単語を語群より選び文章を完成しなさい。

checked
dream
him
reach
worrying

Raymond was a nice young man, but a little too nervous. At bedtime, he was still $_{1}$(　　　　　　) about how to travel on the trains. As I walked past his room, I $_{2}$(　　　　　　) on him because I heard him talking in his sleep. "No no!" "Not a single ... a return! I'm coming back ... but the machine is growing bigger and bigger! I can't $_{3}$(　　　　　　) the buttons! Help! Help!" In the morning, he told me about his $_{4}$(　　　　　　), and I asked $_{5}$(　　　　　　) to draw a picture of it. Here it is.

Unit 15 Airport Forms 関係副詞

Warm-up

次の日本語を参考にして、空所に与えられた文字で始まる単語を書きなさい。

ターミナル　歩道　運動　情報

1. There is some (i　　　　　　　) that tells you what to do and where things are.
2. Walking through an airport is good (e　　　　　　　).
3. Riding on a moving (w　　　　　　　) will save you time.
4. You have to take a bus that transfers you to a distant (t　　　　　　　) building.

1 Reading

CD 37

Every time we change planes, we have to fill in more forms. I will show you (ア) to do it. If you want, I can help you with this one. Can you see item number one? Well, that's (イ) you write your family name. A family name is something like Smith, Brown, or Ford. Under that is where you write your given or first name, like David, Peter, or Samuel. Write your full name. Oh, and you must write those names in capital letters. Don't write that information in cursive script ... you know, like all joined-up. [1]<u>You'll have to print it.</u>

Where did you get your passport from? On this line, write both the country and the state. [2]<u>Be careful about your next answer.</u> The form asks you (ウ) you are visiting this country. If you say [3]<u>it</u> is on business, you'll probably need some evidence like letters and pamphlets. It's (a)(language / same / the / with) study. You'll need a letter proving that you have been accepted to study at a language school. You'll also need a bank statement (b)(have / show / that / to / you) enough money. The form also asks (エ) you are going to leave. It was never this complex when I was your age.

Notes **given name** (=first name)「名前」　**capital letter**「大文字」　**cursive script** (=joined-up)「筆記体」
bank statement「口座取引明細書」

1 ア～エに関係副詞 (when, where, why, how) を書きなさい。

ア. (　　　　　)　イ. (　　　　　)　ウ. (　　　　　)　エ. (　　　　　)

2 本文中の名字と名前以外にそれぞれ 2 つずつ例を挙げなさい。

family name: (　　　　　) (　　　　　)　given name: (　　　　　) (　　　　　)

3 指示に従って書き換えなさい。

1. 下線部 1 を否定文に

2. 下線部 2 を you で始め同じ意味の文に

4 下線部 3 の it の内容を日本語で答えなさい。

5 次の単語の下線部の発音と同じ発音の語をア～エから選びなさい。

1. change	ア. ankle	イ. calm	ウ. date	エ. talk
2. item	ア. knit	イ. mind	ウ. pick	エ. slip
3. accept	ア. cinema	イ. circle	ウ. face	エ. public

6 本文の内容に合うように、空所に与えられた文字で始まる文中の単語を書きなさい。

1. You must write your name in (c　　　　　) letters.
2. On the second line, you must write your (f　　　　　) name.
3. You might need some (e　　　　　) to show what you intend to do in the country.

7 (a) (b) の語を正しく並べ替えなさい。

(a) (language / same / the / with)

(b) (have / show / that / to / you)

2 Conversation

A 日本文を参考にして (　) の語句を正しく並べ替えなさい。ただし文頭に来る語も小文字にしてある。

1. Now, (back / get / let's / this form / to).（さて、この用紙に戻りましょう）

2. (can / find / I / that / where)?（どこでそれを見つけられますか）

3. Then (a slash / answer / in / put / the) space.（それでは回答欄にスラッシュを入れてください）

B **A** の英文 (1) ～ (3) を、適切な空所 (a) ～ (c) に入れて会話を完成しなさい。 CD 38

W: What do I write here? What does this mean? It wants to know my flight number. (　a　)

M: Your flight number is right here. There are two capital letters and a number. Next to it is the gate number. Yours is Gate 23, so simply follow the overhead gate signs and wait in the lounge until your flight is called. (　b　)

W: For this question, I don't have an answer.

M: Right. (　c　) Whatever you do, don't leave it empty.

W: Well, thanks a lot for all your help.

C 質問に対する正しい答えを (A) (B) から選びなさい。

1. What does a flight number look like?
   (A) It has two numbers and one small letter.
   (B) There are two capital letters and one number.

2. What must you do if you have no answer?
   (A) Just leave the answer blank.　　(B) Put a slash in the space.

Grammar　関係副詞

1. 関係副詞の働き

・接続詞＋副詞の働き（＝前置詞＋関係代名詞）

The village **in which** I was born is beautiful. ＜前置詞＋関係代名詞＞

The village **which** I was born **in** is beautiful. （私が生まれた村は美しいです）

The village where I was born is beautiful. ＜関係副詞＞

☞ in +which は関係副詞 where で置き換えることができます。

2. 関係副詞の使い方

・先行詞によって、どの関係副詞を使うかが決まります。

This is **the airport** where Monica works. ＜先行詞が場所＞

（これはモニカが働いている空港です）

I remember **the day** when I visited the town. ＜先行詞が時＞

（その町を訪れた日を覚えています）

That is (**the reason**) why Lisa texts her mother every day. ＜先行詞が理由＞

（それはリサが毎日母に携帯メールを出す理由です）

This is (**the way**) how I write messages. ＜先行詞が方法＞

（私はこうやってメッセージを書きます）

☞ the way か how か、どちらか一方を省略します。

Unit 16 During the Flight

1 Reading

Your flight number is here, on the right, Grandma. It's just like with a bus. Every bus needs a route number and it's the same here. The flight number usually has two or three letters and two or three numbers. This is it here. The gate is where we actually get on the plane.

Now, let's get back to this form. For this question, there's no answer, so put a slash or write ... "none" ... in the answer space. Also, as I've told you before, don't fold your ticket. There's another number that you need to know. That's your seat number. The first bit is the row number, and the A, B, etc. is the seat number. You're in A by the window, so you'll have a good view of taking off and landing. Put your papers — that is, your ticket, passport, and boarding pass — in your pocket or handbag. The things that you don't need during the flight should go into your hand luggage, which will be stored in the overhead bin.

Notes **first bit**「最初の桁」 **row number**「列番号」 **boarding pass**「搭乗券」 **hand luggage**「手荷物」 **overhead bin**「頭上の荷物ラック」

1 次の単語の意味を (a) ～ (e) から選び、下線上にその記号を書きなさい。

1. route ____
2. actually ____
3. form ____
4. slash ____
5. land ____

(a) a document with spaces for filling in information
(b) a short, straight line
(c) a way to get from one place to another place
(d) in a true or factual way
(e) to come back down onto the ground after a flight

2 次の英文が本文の内容に合っていれば T、違っていれば F を選びなさい。

1. A flight number is similar to a bus's route number. T F
2. An airport gate is where you board the plane. T F
3. Grandma's seat is next to the aisle. T F

2 Conversation

A 会話を聞いて空所に単語を書きなさい。 CD 40

M: Did you know that we need a visa to get into the United States?

W: I wonder why?

M: And that's not all. When we get to the US $_1$(　　　　　　　　), we have to put all our information into a computer yet again.

W: How do most passengers $_2$(　　　　　　　　) about that?

M: Pretty angry, because it takes almost an hour to get $_3$(　　　　　　　　) the computer checkpoint.

W: Isn't there a $_4$(　　　　　　　　) way to do it?

B 質問を聞いて空所に単語を書き、適切な答えを (A) (B) から選びなさい。 CD 41

1. What causes the long (　　　　　　　　) at US airports?
   (A) Putting personal data into computers.　　(B) The flights are always full.

2. How long does it take to (　　　　　　　　) your data when you visit the US?
   (A) About an hour.　　(B) Half an hour.

3 Short Talk

イラストを見ながら、空所に入る単語を語群より選び文章を完成しなさい。

arch
remove
shoes
take
using

Walk through the $_1$(　　　　　　　　), please. Ah, the alarm went off. Could you walk through again? Oh, $_2$(　　　　　　　　) off your jacket, please. That's the alarm again. Once more, but $_3$(　　　　　　　　) any other thick clothing — like that heavy sweater. Sorry, alarm again. Once more, sir, but no $_4$(　　　　　　　　), please. Now, where are my glasses? I was $_5$(　　　　　　　　) them a few minutes ago. I must have dropped them somewhere.

Unit 17 What kind of person? 不定詞・動名詞

Warm-up

次の日本語を参考にして、空所に与えられた文字で始まる単語を書きなさい。

重要な　群衆　スピーチ　見る

1. The man is making a (s　　　　　) on the street.
2. There is quite a large (c　　　　　) here.
3. Maybe we will (s　　　　　) this man on TV as an (i　　　　　) leader someday.

1 Reading

CD 42

I have got to evaluate that young man, and then the committee will decide whether [ア](hire) him or not. Well, what's my first impression? [1]He looks good. His clothes and hair are tidy. He wants [イ](be) a salesman. I am not too keen on people's long hair or tattoos, but he has none of [2]that stuff. Next, I'll find out how he speaks. Well, that is a pleasant surprise. He is very polite and takes the other person into consideration. [3]That is just the sort of person we've been looking for.

He can drive and got his licence five years ago. [4]It seems that he is a very good driver. He says that he drives carefully and that he has a clean licence except for a couple of parking tickets. Because he speaks so politely, he should fit in nicely with our home-delivery service.

I've been trying to get our staff [ウ](improve) their corporate image. We now actually enjoy [エ](wear) smart clothes, [オ](put) on a nice tie, [(a)](forgetting / not / smile / to), and saying thank you. I think that young man can [(b)](all / do / without / that) any trouble.

Notes **be keen on**「～が好きである」 **take ... into consideration**「～を配慮する」 **sort of person**「～のような人」 **clean licence**「違反のない運転免許証」 **parking ticket**「駐車違反切符」

1 ア～オの単語を不定詞か動名詞にして書きなさい。

ア. (　　　　　)　イ. (　　　　　)　ウ. (　　　　　)

エ. (　　　　　)　オ. (　　　　　)

2 指示に従って書き換えなさい。

1. 下線部 1 の good を問う疑問文に

2. 下線部 4 を He seems で始めて

3 下線部 2 の that stuff の具体的な内容を日本語で答えなさい。

4 下線部 3 の That の具体的な内容を日本語で答えなさい。

5 次の単語の最も強く発音する箇所を答えなさい。

1. com・mit・tee
   ア　イ　ウ
2. im・pres・sion
   ア　イ　ウ
3. tat・too
   ア　イ
4. con・sid・er・a・tion
   ア　イ　ウ　エ　オ
5. im・prove
   ア　イ
6. cor・po・rate
   ア　イ　ウ

6 本文の内容に合うように、空所に与えられた文字で始まる文中の単語を書きなさい。

1. She first noticed that the young man's clothes and hair are both (t　　　　　).
2. He is very (p　　　　　) when he speaks to people.
3. He hasn't had any real (t　　　　　) driving his car.

7 (a) (b) の語を正しく並べ替えなさい。

(a) (forgetting / not / smile / to)

(b) (all / do / without / that)

2 Conversation

A 日本文を参考にして（　）内の語句を正しく並べ替えなさい。ただし文頭に来る語も小文字にしてある。

1. (a computer / can / use / you)?（コンピュータを使えますか）

2. No, I (about / know / things / to / want) you enjoyed learning.
   （いいえ、あなたが楽しく学んだことについて知りたいのです）

3. Now, (can / me / tell / what / you) you enjoyed in school?
   （さて、学校で何が楽しかったか話してくれますか）

B **A** の英文 (1) ～ (3) を、適切な空所 (a) ～ (c) に入れて会話を完成しなさい。 CD 43

M: Sit down, please. (a)

W: Do you mean things like clubs and friends?

M: (b)

W: English, and writing short stories.

M: (c)

W: Yes. I pick up new programs fairly quickly and so I will be a valuable asset.

C 質問に対する正しい答えを (A) (B) から選びなさい。

1. How did the woman handle the man's first question?
   (A) She answered it correctly right away.
   (B) She misunderstood the question.

2. Why most likely will she become a good worker?
   (A) Because she can use a computer and learns quickly.
   (B) Because she joined many clubs and has lots of friends.

Grammar 不定詞・動名詞

1. 不定詞の用法

☞ 名詞的用法、形容詞的用法、副詞的用法

To go to law school is Sam's hope.（ロースクールに行くことはサムの希望です）

Helen has an assignment to do.（ヘレンはするべき課題があります）

Eric went to New York to study business administration.
（エリックは経営学を学ぶためにニューヨークへ行きました）

2. 動名詞の用法

☞ 動詞の原形に -ing で、主語、補語、目的語、前置詞の目的語の働き

Getting information from the internet is efficient.
（インターネットで情報を得ることは効率的です）

Young people love using SNS.（若い人は SNS を使うのが好きです）

3. 不定詞のみを目的語にとる動詞、動名詞のみを目的語にとる動詞

不定詞：afford, agree, claim, decide, plan, refuse, want, wish, etc.
動名詞：avoid, deny, enjoy, finish, give up, mind, miss, resist, etc.

Heather **decided** to buy a pair of shoes.（ヘザーは靴を買うことに決めました）

Robert **enjoyed** reading the book.（ロバートは本を読むのを楽しみました）

4. 不定詞と動名詞で意味が異なる動詞：forget, remember, regret, stop など

Remember to call her tomorrow night.「忘れずに～する」
（明日の夜、忘れずに彼女に電話をしてください）

Mary **remembers** seeing him.「～したことを覚えている」
（メアリは彼に会ったことを覚えています）

Unit 18 At the Hotel

1 Reading

10 CD 44

Brendan Snowdon has been a travelling salesman since he left university. Most days he drives to the next city, sees a couple of clients, gets his next orders, uploads them to his main office's computer, and then tries to relax at his next hotel. It is a tiring job, and it annoys him when people make mistakes. At this hotel, things are going quite badly. He has spent one night there so far and has booked for a second night, but, well, let's listen and find out what's bothering Brendan.

He went to the reception desk this morning, and the staff member there said, "Yes, sir. May I help you?" Brendan said he had checked in the night before and spent one night there. However, he wasn't able to use the room's phone because it didn't work. He wanted the hotel to fix it right away. But Brendan hadn't finished. He then explained that room service had left a bathroom set of soap, shampoo, etc., but that there was no razor and no towels.

The hotel man was visibly shaken by Brendan's complaints. He promised that while Brendan was having breakfast, the cleaning staff and an engineer would be working on his poorly serviced room.

Notes **so far**「今のところ」 **book for a second night**「２泊目を予約する」 **right away**「すぐに」 **cleaning staff**「清掃係」 **poorly serviced**「サービスの不十分な」

1 次の単語の意味を (a) ～ (e) から選び、下線上にその記号を書きなさい。

1. client _____
2. upload _____
3. fix _____
4. complaint _____
5. visibly _____

(a) a statement that something is wrong
(b) a customer who receives service
(c) easily seen or understood
(d) to move a file or information onto a computer
(e) to repair something

2 次の英文が本文の内容に合っていれば T、違っていれば F を選びなさい。

1. Brendan has worked at several different jobs. T F
2. He is scheduled to stay two nights at this hotel. T F
3. The hotel is taking Brendan's complaints seriously. T F

2 Conversation

A 会話を聞いて空所に単語を書きなさい。 CD 45

M: Just look at these cars! Aren't they great? A classy sedan just right for a sophisticated woman! And an open-top car that is very 1(　　　　　　) to drive.

W: Gosh, I can't make up my mind. Tell me some more about them.

M: Well, with this classy model, you roll up the windows, turn on the air conditioner, and drive in comfort and 2(　　　　　　).

W: That sounds perfect for me. But what 3(　　　　　　) the other one?

M: Just put it in gear and you fly like a rocket as people watch your hair 4(　　　　　　) in the wind. I personally love this sort of car. So much fun to drive!

W: How much is it? I presume it's not as expensive as the other one.

B 質問を聞いて空所に単語を書き、適切な答えを (A) (B) から選びなさい。 CD 46

1. How does the woman feel about the (　　　　　　) car?
   (A) She thinks it is just what she wanted.
   (B) She thinks it is not her cup of tea.

2. How does the man feel about the (　　　　　　) car?
   (A) He thinks driving it is very exciting.
   (B) He thinks it might be too expensive for the woman.

3 Short Talk

イラストを見ながら、空所に入る単語を語群より選び文章を完成しなさい。

before
looking
mess
that
wearing

You'd better be really careful when you choose your next car. For example, a luxury model has an aura about it 1(　　　　　　) you have respect for. See that dark blue car over there. Can you pop down to the shops 2(　　　　　　) rough jeans and an old T-shirt driving that? No way! You have to get all dressed up 3(　　　　　　) you can drive a car like that. And what about this little red one? You get in 4(　　　　　　) beautiful, but in no time your lovely hair will be a 5(　　　　　　) and your make-up will be ruined!

Unit 19 Driving Instructions　形容詞・副詞

Warm-up

次の日本語を参考にして、空所に与えられた文字で始まる単語を書きなさい。

ヨーロッパ　道路　国　理解する

1. Can you read this (r　　　　　　　) sign that is in (E　　　　　　　)?
2. I can (u　　　　　　　) the sign's information.
3. Tourists from many (c　　　　　　　) come here, and they need to know where things are.

1 Reading

CD 47

Hello, dear. Nice to meet you. Thank you for the phone call. I looked around the yard to see what we have in, and I can tell you that you've come to the right place. If you want a ア(nicely) secondhand car that is not too expensive, then take a look at [1]this one right here. The interior is clean, (a)(and / is / so / the engine). It is a イ(quietly) car, and for a 1500cc, it has a lot of power. And with this car, we can offer you a loan with a very low rate of interest. You see, I told you we run an ウ(honestly) business here.

Now then, on the phone you said that you've never driven an automatic. Well, [2]it is super エ(easily). Just watch me carefully, and you'll be driving like an expert in no time at all. Put the key right in there. Now check to see if the handbrake is on and the gear lever is in P. Next, press the footbrake, then turn the key. Take off the handbrake. Shift the gear to D, and (b)(are / move / ready / to / you). It's as オ(simply) as that.

Notes **secondhand car**「中古車」　**low rate of interest**「低金利」　**in no time at all**「すぐに」
take off the handbrake「ハンドブレーキを外す」

1 ア〜オの単語を適切な形にしなさい。

ア. (　　　　　)　イ. (　　　　　)　ウ. (　　　　　)　エ. (　　　　　)　オ. (　　　　　)

2 下線部 1 の this one が示すものを日本語で答えなさい。

3 下線部 2 の it の具体的な内容を日本語で答えなさい。

____

4 次の単語の比較級・最上級を書きなさい。

1. expensive (　　　　　　)-(　　　　　　)　2. clean (　　　　)-(　　　　)
3. low (　　　　)-(　　　　)　4. carefully (　　　　　　)-(　　　　　　)
5. simple (　　　　)-(　　　　)

5 次の単語の最も強く発音する箇所を答えなさい。

1. au・to・mat・ic
ア　イ　ウ　エ

2. care・ful・ly
ア　イ　ウ

3. ex・pen・sive
ア　イ　ウ

4. in・ter・est
ア　イ　ウ

5. in・te・ri・or
ア　イ　ウ　エ

6 本文の内容に合うように、空所に与えられた文字で始まる文中の単語を書きなさい。

1. The interior of the secondhand car is very (c　　　　　).
2. The customer can get a low-interest (l　　　　　) with this car.
3. Driving an (a　　　　　　　) car is super easy.

7 (a) (b) の語句を正しく並べ替えなさい。

(a) (and / is / so / the engine)

____

(b) (are / move / ready / to / you)

____

2 Conversation

A 日本文を参考にして (　) 内の語句を正しく並べ替えなさい。ただし文頭に来る語も小文字にしてある。

1. (as / as that / bad / if / it's), I'll probably buy a small but new car.
（そんなに悪いのであれば、おそらく小型の新車を買うでしょう）

____

2. (go / of / sort / things / what) wrong?（どんな悪いことがあるのですか）

____

3. It cracks, and suddenly (a / huge / making / noise / starts).
（ひびが入り、突然大きな音が発生します）

____

CD 48

B **A** の英文 (1) ～ (3) を、適切な空所 (a) ～ (c) に入れて会話を完成しなさい。

M: Driving a secondhand car is great, that is, if nothing goes wrong.

W: What do you mean? (a)

M: The muffler gets rusty. (b)

W: What else?

M: Starting the engine in the morning becomes difficult especially in winter.

W: (c)

C 質問に対する正しい答えを (A) (B) から選びなさい。

1. How does the man feel about buying a used car?
   (A) He says usually there are no problems at all.
   (B) It seems as if you are just buying trouble.

2. What will the woman most likely do?
   (A) She will buy a more expensive secondhand car.
   (B) She will buy a new compact car.

Grammar　形容詞・副詞

形容詞の働き

☞ 限定的用法：名詞の前に置いて名詞を修飾
☞ 叙述的用法：主語＋ be 動詞＋形容詞

Anne bought a new **car** recently.（アンは最近新しい車を買いました）

This car **is** economical.（この車は経済的です）

I want to drink **something** cold.（何か冷たいものを飲みたいです）

☞ something のように -thing の場合は形容詞を後ろに置きます。

副詞の働き

☞ 動詞・形容詞・副詞・文全体を修飾

Michael still **remembers** the event vividly.
（マイケルはまだそのイベントをはっきりと覚えています）

Laura bought surprisingly **expensive** shoes.（ローラは驚くほど値段の高い靴を買いました）

Luckily, **this suit fits Bob perfectly**.（運良く、このスーツはボブにピッタリです）

比較表現

1. 同等比較：as ＋形容詞・副詞の原級＋ as

Jessica speaks Spanish **as** well **as** Chinese.
（ジェシカは中国語と同じぐらい上手にスペイン語を話します）

2. 比較級：比較級＋ than

My car is more convenient **than** I thought.（私の車は思っていたよりも便利です）

3. 最上級：the ＋最上級

David is the most reliable friend in my class.
（ディビッドはクラスで最も信頼できる友だちです）

Unit 20 A Lovely Blouse

1 Reading

11 CD 49

When I finished work yesterday, I took the bus into town to meet Jenny. I got there on time and waited for her, but then she texted me saying that she would be an hour late. I was wondering how to kill the time, when I saw some lovely blouses in the window of the High Street Gap. I went in and before I knew it, a perky young salesgirl was chatting with me and showing me a new blouse.

She even said that if I didn't buy this blouse now, I would never forgive myself. I looked at some others and tried one on. It was beautiful but too tight under my arms because I've been putting on weight since the end of summer. The perky salesgirl brought me a larger one, which fitted perfectly, so I bought it.

I left and did a bit more window shopping and then met up with Jenny. We went into that new pub-restaurant near the Town Hall. It was warm in there, so we took off our coats. Jenny looked great and fashionable, but guess what she was wearing!

Notes **kill the time**「時間をつぶす」 **before I know it**「いつの間にか」 **try ... on**「～を試着する」 **put on weight**「体重が増える」 **take off**「脱ぐ」

1 次の単語の意味を (a) ～ (e) から選び、下線上にその記号を書きなさい。

1. text ____
2. perky ____
3. chat ____
4. tight ____
5. fashionable ____

(a) trendy or stylish
(b) fitting very close to your body
(c) lively and energetic
(d) to send someone a message by a cellphone
(e) to talk with someone in a casual way

2 次の英文が本文の内容に合っていれば T、違っていれば F を選びなさい。

1. Jenny telephoned to say that she would be half an hour late. T F
2. The first blouse the salesgirl brought was too large. T F
3. Jenny was dressed nicely and looked attractive. T F

2 Conversation

A 会話を聞いて空所に単語を書きなさい。 CD 50

W: Now then, I want to look at the new autumn dresses.

M: If you are going to do that, I'll go to the men's $_1$(   ) section and see if I can find a nice long-sleeved shirt.

W: That's fine. I'll phone you when I have $_2$(   ). See you later.

....

W: Wow! You have a $_3$(   ) of shopping there. What did you buy?

M: They had some great bargains at half price.

W: Why was everything so $_4$(   )?

M: It was the last day of the summer sale. So I bought half a dozen shirts.

B 質問を聞いて空所に単語を書き、適切な答えを (A) (B) から選びなさい。 CD 51

1. What kind of (   ) did the man do?
   (A) He bought a long-sleeved sweater.   (B) He bought several shirts.

2. Why did he buy so many of (   )?
   (A) They were on sale fifty percent off.   (B) They were all just the right size.

3 Short Talk

イラストを見ながら、空所に入る単語を語群より選び文章を完成しなさい。

feet
giveaway
happens
load
pop

All the summer things are really at $_1$(   ) prices right now. When you walk past a shop window, how do you feel? I don't know about you, but my $_2$(   ) suddenly stand still, and I can't move. I usually $_3$(   ) in to look at the bargains but walk out with a $_4$(   ) of full bags. My daughter can't understand what $_5$(   ) to me when I am on a shopping trip. I don't understand it either, but it is a lot of fun.

Unit 21 How was your room? 疑問詞・未来形

Warm-up

次の日本語を参考にして、空所に与えられた文字で始まる単語を書きなさい。

シャワー　木　眺め　夢見る

1. The (v　　　　　) from my hotel room was perfect.
2. There were tall palm (t　　　　　), and in the distance was the beautiful sea. This was what I had (d　　　　　) of.
3. Beware when you turn on the (s　　　　　)! Make sure hot water comes out.

1 Reading

CD 52

I had just finished my breakfast, and I was ①(about) leave the dining room, when someone behind me said, "Hello, madam. [1]<u>We are doing a survey</u> to try to find out what our guests think of the hotel. (ア) will you check out? If you agree to the survey, it ②(take) only a couple of minutes, and it ③(help) us to reorganise the hotel." [2]<u>I had plenty of time that day</u>, so I answered "OK."

"(イ) do you want to know?" I asked. The first question was ... "How was your room?" Well, I had lots to say. It's a nice room with a great view from the window, but it was too noisy with so many people using the elevator late at night. I wonder (ウ) you don't switch it off after midnight. Also, (エ) cleans the room? And do you know that room has a damp and musty smell? The air conditioner filter needs changing, and you should hang out the bedding on a fine day. (オ) long do the cleaners spend polishing things? If they (a)(10 / more / spend / would) minutes, the room would be more comfortable. If you do all that, your guests ④(going) to have a lovely stay. Maybe I said too much, but the woman did say, "Well, thank (b)(for / very much / views / you / your)."

Notes　**switch ... off**「～のスイッチを切る」　**damp and musty**「湿ってかび臭い」　**hang out**「干す」　**bedding**「寝具」

1 ア～オに疑問詞 (who, when, what, why, how) を書きなさい。

ア. (　　　　　)　イ. (　　　　　)　ウ. (　　　　　)　エ. (　　　　　)　オ. (　　　　　)

2 ①～④の単語を使って未来形にしなさい。

① (　　　　　　)　② (　　　　　　)　③ (　　　　　　)　④ (　　　　　　)

3 次の文中の単語と同じ意味の語を (a) ～ (e) をから選びなさい。

1. views (　　)　2. survey (　　)　3. polish (　　)　4. cleaner (　　)　5. reorganise (　　)

(a) change　(b) clean　(c) maid　(d) opinion　(e) study

4 指示に従って書き換えなさい。

1. 下線部 1 の survey を問う疑問文に

____

2. 下線部 2 の that day を tomorrow に換えて未来形の文に

____

5 次の語の下線部の発音と同じ発音の語をア～エから選びなさい。

1. finished	ア. looked	イ. needed	ウ. surprised	エ. opened
2. leave	ア. breath	イ. feature	ウ. pleasure	エ. sweat
3. behind	ア. chip	イ. machine	ウ. minister	エ. polite

6 本文の内容に合うように、空所に与えられた文字で始まる文中の単語を書きなさい。

1. The hotel guest has enough (t　　　　　) to talk to the staff today.
2. The guest's room was a good one but it was too (n　　　　　).
3. The bad (s　　　　　) came from different things in the room.

7 (a) (b) の語句を正しく並べ替えなさい。

(a) (10 / more / spend / would)

____

(b) (for / very much / views / you / your)

____

2 Conversation

A 日本文を参考にして (　　) の語句を正しく並べ替えなさい。ただし文頭に来る語も小文字にしてある。

1. (be / coming / could / from / it) the engine and getting into the car through a hole.
(それはエンジンから出て、穴を通って車の中に入っているのかもしれません)

____

2. Well, (come / I / think of / to / when) it, yes, I did. (ええ、考えてみると、はい、そうでした)

____

3. It started last summer and (bad / hot / on / quite / was) days.
(それは昨年の夏から始まり、暑い日はとてもひどかったです)

____

B **A** の英文 (1) ～ (3) を、適切な空所 (a) ～ (c) に入れて会話を完成しなさい。 CD 53

W: Can you find out what is causing that strange smell in my car, and then fix it?

M: (　a　) Or it might be someone's body smell, like sweat or cigarettes.

W: (　b　)

M: Ah, I think I know the reason. Did you change your hair spray in summer?

W: (　c　)

M: That's easy to fix. Just throw the hair spray away.

C 質問に対する正しい答えを (A) (B) から選びなさい。

1. How long did it take the man to find the cause of the smell?
   (A) He is still looking for it.　　(B) It didn't take long.

2. What caused the smell?
   (A) Hair spray.　　(B) Sweat and cigarettes.

Grammar　疑問詞・未来形

疑問詞

☞ 疑問詞は文頭に来て、人、場所、時間、理由、方法などを尋ねるときに用います。

疑問詞	意味	尋ねること
what	何	もの
who	誰	人
where	どこ	場所
when	いつ	時
why	なぜ	理由
how	どのように	方法

1. who が主語のとき Who + 動詞？

Who runs fast?（誰が速く走りますか）— Eric does.（エリックです）

☞ 疑問詞が主語のとき、肯定文の語順で do/does は使いません。
who は主語になると 3 人称扱いなので動詞に -s を付けます。

2. who が目的語のとき Who + 疑問文（be 動詞＋主語 , do/does/did ＋主語＋動詞）?

Who is the woman over there?（向こうの女性は誰ですか）

Who do you live with?（あなたは誰と住んでいますか）

未来形

1. will の使い方

☞ 今決めたこと、不確実な未来の予測　＜**will ＋動詞の原形**＞

I will book a new hotel by the sea.（海辺の新しいホテルを予約します）

Beth will have a great time with her friends.（ベスは友人と楽しい時間を過ごすでしょう）

2. be going to の使い方

☞ すでに決まっている予定や、確実に起こりそうなこと　＜**be going to ＋動詞の原形**＞

We are going to go out for dinner tomorrow.（私たちは明日ディナーに出かけます）

Kevin is going to arrive at the hotel at 5:00 p.m.（ケビンは午後 5 時にホテルに着きます）

Unit 22 What happened?

1 Reading

12 54

When I got home from work yesterday evening, I changed into something comfortable, and then I walked to the shops. When I got there, I saw a yellow double-decker bus coming down the hill. It was going quite fast and didn't stop at the traffic lights. It hit that blue car. That one over there. Then, both the drivers got out and started shouting at each other. I thought they were going to get into a real fight! But just then a patrol car came by and stopped, and one of the policemen got out.

The bus driver suddenly changed into a quiet, polite person. Even though it was a bad accident, I couldn't help laughing. The car needed a new front end and one side was badly damaged, and the bus was dented at the front. I'm sure it was the bus driver's fault. He should have stopped at the bottom of the hill, but he just kept going without braking. Perhaps he had fallen asleep, or he might have been talking or even texting on his smartphone. It was lucky that no one was hurt.

Notes **change into**「～に着替える」 **double-decker**「ダブルデッカー」2 階建てのバス **traffic light**「交通信号」 **patrol car**「パトカー」 **can't help -ing**「～せざるをえない」

1 次の単語の意味を (a) ～ (e) から選び、下線上にその記号を書きなさい。

1. comfortable _____
2. fight _____
3. dented _____
4. fault _____
5. bottom _____

(a) casual and easy to wear
(b) responsibility for a problem; blame
(c) the lowest part of something
(d) an angry argument
(e) having a hollow mark in the surface caused by a hit

2 次の英文が本文の内容に合っていれば T、違っていれば F を選びなさい。

1. The bus crashed into the train.	T	F
2. The drivers were really fighting when the police arrived.	T	F
3. It seems as if the bus driver hadn't been concentrating on driving.	T	F

2 Conversation

A 会話を聞いて空所に単語を書きなさい。 CD 55

W: How long have you been driving buses?

M: I got my bus licence when I was $_{1}$(　　　　　　　), and I've been a bus driver ever since.

W: What's changed in your $_{2}$(　　　　　　　) over the years?

M: We used to have a lot of trouble with $_{3}$(　　　　　　　) at night.

W: Why did you say "used to"?

M: Well, now most people have $_{4}$(　　　　　　　) with cameras. This has stopped a lot of the abuse.

B 質問を聞いて空所に単語を書き、適切な答えを (A) (B) から選びなさい。 CD 56

1. How (　　　　　　　) has the man been driving buses?
   (A) For twenty years.　　(B) Since he was twenty.

2. What seems to have (　　　　　　　) in his work?
   (A) Drivers have less trouble at night than in the past.
   (B) Large buses are a lot easier to drive.

3 Short Talk

イラストを見ながら、空所に入る単語を語群より選び文章を完成しなさい。

coming
corner
fast
traffic
vehicles

[Accident report]

I was walking uphill from the lights on Cherry Tree Road, when I saw a yellow bus $_{1}$(　　　　　　　) down the hill. I'm sure the bus was going too $_{2}$(　　　　　　　). The bus driver braked too late at the bottom of the hill, just in front of the $_{3}$(　　　　　　　) lights. A blue car had just come round the $_{4}$(　　　　　　　) into Cherry Tree Road. The bus hit the car. Nobody was injured, fortunately, but both $_{5}$(　　　　　　　) were badly damaged.

Unit 23 Shopping　可算名詞・不可算名詞

Warm-up

次の日本語を参考にして、空所に与えられた文字で始まる単語を書きなさい。

看板　予算　着る　よく知られている

1. It is a cold day, and the people are (w　　　　　　　　) something warm.
2. Another thing is making the shoppers happy. That is the shops' (s　　　　　　　).
3. They are easy to read and (f　　　　　　　　) to most young people.
4. Go inside and look around. Check the prices and see if they are within your (b　　　　　　　).

1 Reading

CD 57

Hmm. Something that I really don't want to do but I have to do is ... shopping. I need some fruit, and half a dozen ア(apple / apples) and five or six oranges should be enough. I don't have any イ(milk / milks), so I'd better get some. Two litres should last until the weekend. Is there any ウ(rice / rices) in the kitchen? I don't think so. [1]That means I'll have to get a lot of items, and that's going to be heavy.

Tomorrow, I'm planning to make a vegetarian dinner for two friends. I'll need quite a few エ(egg / eggs) for the omelette, so I'll pick up two packs. For breakfast, I'll need one loaf of オ(bread / breads) and some coffee powder. I won't have much time to make a lunch box in the morning, so [2]I had better buy a ready-made lunch. This one looks OK. It doesn't have much カ(meat / meats), and (a)(are / different / several / there) vegetables in [3]it, so (b)(another / problem / solved / that's). As I told you, I don't like shopping.

Notes　**quite a few**「かなりたくさんの」　**pick up**「買う」　**coffee powder**「コーヒー粉」
lunch box「お弁当」　**ready-made**「出来合いの」

1 ア〜カの正しい単語を選びなさい。

ア. (　　　　　)　イ. (　　　　　)　ウ. (　　　　　)　エ. (　　　　　)　オ. (　　　　　)　カ. (　　　　　)

2 下線部 1 の That の具体的な内容を日本語で答えなさい。

____

3 下線部 2 のように思った理由を日本語で答えなさい。

____

4 下線部 3 の it の内容を日本語で答えなさい。

____

5 次の単語の最も強く発音する箇所を答えなさい。

1. or・ange
   ア　イ
2. week・end
   ア　イ
3. om・e・lette
   ア　イ　ウ
4. veg・e・tar・i・an
   ア　イ　ウ　エ　オ
5. veg・e・ta・ble
   ア　イ　ウ　エ

6 本文の内容に合うように、空所に与えられた文字で始まる文中の単語を書きなさい。

1. The woman goes out (s　　　　　) because she has to.
2. She is going to buy two (l　　　　　) of milk.
3. She can save (t　　　　　) today by buying a lunch box.

7 (a) (b) の語を正しく並べ替えなさい。

(a) (are / different / several / there)

____

(b) (another / problem / solved / that's)

____

2 Conversation

A 日本文を参考にして（　）の語を正しく並べ替えなさい。ただし文頭に来る語も小文字にしてある。

1. (are / going / to / what / you) have?（何を飲みますか）

____

2. (a / beer / cold / have / I'll).（僕は冷えたビールにします）

____

3. I can't (believe / hot / how / is / it) today.（今日は信じられないほど暑いですね）

____

CD 58

B **A** の英文 (1) ～ (3) を、適切な空所 (a) ～ (c) に入れて会話を完成しなさい。

W: Let's go into that coffee shop and sit down for a while.

M: Yes. (a)

W: I guess a shop like this one is making a fortune.

M: (b)

W: I think I'll go for some ice cream and a coke.

M: (c)

C 質問に対する正しい答えを (A) (B) から選びなさい。

1. Why do they want to go into the coffee shop?
   (A) It is lunchtime. (B) It is so hot today.

2. What did the man order?
   (A) Cold beer. (B) Ice cream.

Grammar 可算名詞・不可算名詞

可算名詞（数えられる名詞）

1. 普通名詞 (car, table, kitchen, etc.)

☞ 不定冠詞 (a / an)、定冠詞 (the) が付くか、または複数形になります。

Is there a **supermarket** nearby?（近くにスパーマーケットがありますか）

Alex bought a **laptop** yesterday.（アレックスは昨日ノートパソコンを買いました）

The **books** on the **shelf** are often used.（棚の上の本はよく使用されます）

2. 集合名詞 (family, team, police, etc.)

The **family** are all well.（家族はみんな元気です）

The **police** are coming into the store.（警察がその店に入って来ています）

不可算名詞（数えられない名詞）

1. 固有名詞 (Finland, Smith, etc.), 物質名詞 (coffee, sugar, etc.), 抽象名詞 (information, truth, etc.)

☞ advice, baggage, luggage, furniture, health, knowledge, news, beer, tea, honesty, etc. は不可算名詞なので不定冠詞 (a / an) をつけたり複数形にしたりしません。

× Can you give me some advices?
○ Can you give me some advice?（アドバイスをくれますか）

× I have a good news.
○ I have good news.（良い知らせがあります）

2. 不可算名詞の数え方

Carol is collecting **a bit of** information.（キャロルは少し情報を集めています）

I drank **two cups of** coffee for lunch.（ランチでコーヒーを 2 杯飲みました）

☞ **a bottle of** wine, **a glass of** juice, **a piece of** cake, **a sheet of** paper, **a pair of** glasses, etc.

Unit 24 Street Directions

1 Reading

13 CD 59

Jenny has been a friend of mine for lots of years; since school, in fact, I like her very much, but she has one fault. She talks and talks. That's Jenny over there. I wonder if you can hear her? She has lost her way and is trying to find the Union Bank. She is asking a middle-aged man how to get there. "Excuse me, sir. I'm sorry to trouble you, but I wonder if you can help me. I've been driving round in circles for half an hour trying to find the Union Bank."

And then she kept talking, as usual. "Do you know where it is? I've got to send some money to a bank in Hawaii. You see, I bought some land there, and I want to build a house on the plot. The problem is that someone must look after the empty lot. The city is about to fine me because the weeds on the lot are growing too high. So I must get to the bank to send some money to hire someone ..." The man broke in. "A bank, huh? The only bank around here that I know of is back the way you came. Turn left at the lights, and the bank is on the corner on your left and next to a little pizza shop." Jenny was about to say something else. But the man quickly walked away.

Notes **in fact**「実際」 **lose one's way**「道に迷う」 **drive round in circles**「車でぐるぐる同じところを走る」 **as usual**「いつものように」 **look after**「世話をする」 **break in**「話をさえぎる」

1 次の単語の意味を (a) ～ (e) から選び、下線上にその記号を書きなさい。

1. fault _____
2. plot _____
3. empty _____
4. weed _____
5. hire _____

(a) a bad part of someone's character
(b) a plant that grows quickly where it is not wanted
(c) a piece of land that is used for a particular purpose
(d) not being used
(e) to employ someone for wages

2 次の英文が本文の内容に合っていれば T、違っていれば F を選びなさい。

1. Jenny doesn't know when to stop talking. T F
2. The man did not know any of the banks. T F
3. The man left before Jenny could start talking again. T F

2 Conversation

A 会話を聞いて空所に単語を書きなさい。 CD 60

M: On Monday, I have to go to Boston on business and then go somewhere $_{1}$(　　　　　) Swan Valley. What's the best way to get there?

W: There's a train to Boston, but the buses are more $_{2}$(　　　　　).

M: And how about to the Swan place?

W: My $_{3}$(　　　　　) is that you'll have to drive there.

M: How long does it take and which road is the $_{4}$(　　　　　)?

W: You can get that information from road maps and your GPS.

B 質問を聞いて空所に単語を書き、適切な答えを (A) (B) から選びなさい。 CD 61

1. How does the man (　　　　　) about Swan Valley?
   (A) He is familiar with the place.
   (B) He knows nothing at all about it.

2. Which of the (　　　　　) is true?
   (A) The man will probably go to Swan Valley by car.
   (B) The man will probably take a train to Swan Valley.

3 Short Talk

イラストを見ながら、空所に入る単語を語群より選び文章を完成しなさい。

entrance
lefts
opposite
stand
two

You can usually get a taxi on the next road. Go up this road, and turn left. Go down the hill, and I think you make two $_{1}$(　　　　　), but I'm not too sure about that. It's easy to find, because there's a taxi $_{2}$(　　　　　) on your left, near a bus stop. On the $_{3}$(　　　　　) side of the road, there's a beautiful old $_{4}$(　　　　　) to a garden. You can see $_{5}$(　　　　　) tall trees there.

Unit 25 My Luxury　there 構文・使役動詞

Warm-up

次の日本語を参考にして、空所に与えられた文字で始まる単語を書きなさい。

歩道　露店　雑談する　買い物

1. I wonder why she stopped here to do her (s　　　　　　).
2. The young man's (s　　　　　　) is outside. He spends a few minutes (c　　　　　　) about his fruit with each customer.
3. Even though his shop is on the (p　　　　　　), it is a warm and friendly place.

1 Reading

CD 62

I look at my face in the mirror, and I see something unusual. [1]<u>It</u> is a smile. Not a big, toothy smile, but just a small one. [2]<u>It</u> means that it is Friday evening and I can relax at home until Monday morning. I've finished dinner, but cooking a meal by yourself, for yourself, is never very tasty. Oh well, I sit down, pick up the remote, and check out a couple of programs. I'm sitting in the living room watching the TV. [3]<u>This</u> is my luxury ... a couple of days with nothing to do. It allows me ① (relax / to relax).

To make me ② (feel / to feel) even happier, I think I'll make a nice cup of coffee. I open the cupboard door. There (ア) two coffee cups, and there (イ) some sugar in the corner. Now what about cream? I thought there (ウ) some, but it seems there (エ) not any. I guess I'll have to have black coffee. Here's the coffee powder tin. I wonder how much there (オ) inside. Oh no! I can't believe it. This is not my lucky day. There's enough for just one cup, but not enough for a second one. What can I do about it? I could (a)(a coat / and / go / on / put) to the corner shop. But it is really cold outside today and that would spoil my "luxury" holiday feeling. So I'll have to (b)(and / indoors / go / stay / without) my coffee. Oh, I hate it when this happens!

Notes　**a big, toothy smile**「歯を見せた満面の笑み」　**by oneself**「1人で」　**remote**「リモコン」
This is not my lucky day.「今日はついていない」　**corner shop**「小さな商店」

1 ア〜オに be 動詞 (is, are, was) を入れて、there 構文を完成しなさい。

ア. (　　　　　)　イ. (　　　　　)　ウ. (　　　　　)　エ. (　　　　　)　オ. (　　　　　)

2 ①② の正しいものを選び、文を完成しなさい。

① (　　　　　　　)　② (　　　　　　　)

3 下線部 1 の It が表す内容を日本語で書きなさい。

____

4 下線部 2 の It が表す内容を日本語で書きなさい。

____

5 下線部 3 の This が表す内容を日本語で書きなさい。

____

6 次の語の下線部の発音と同じ発音の語をア〜エから選びなさい。

	ア	イ	ウ	エ
1. finished	ア. attended	イ. laughed	ウ. returned	エ. visited
2. meal	ア. bread	イ. head	ウ. ready	エ. seat
3. enough	ア. fight	イ. light	ウ. tough	エ. through

7 本文の内容に合うように、空所に与えられた文字で始まる文中の単語を書きなさい。

1. His (f　　　　　) looks happy because his holiday is starting.
2. The man seems to be (h　　　　　) at the weekend than on weekdays.
3. It is cold (o　　　　　), so he doesn't want to go to the corner shop.

8 (a) (b) の語句を正しく並べ替えなさい。

(a) (a coat / and / go / on / put)

____

(b) (and / indoors / go / stay / without)

____

2 Conversation

A 日本文を参考にして (　　) の語句を正しく並べ替えなさい。ただし文頭に来る語も小文字にしてある。

1. I think (his first / it / time / to talk / was) to a foreigner other than his teachers.
(彼が先生以外の外国人と話をするのは初めてだったと思います)

____

2. Well, the flight attendant (a cup / brought / coffee / him / of) and said, "Here you go, sir." (ええ、客室乗務員が彼に一杯のコーヒーを持ってきて、「はい、どうぞ」と言いました)

____

3. (drink / something / to)? (何か飲み物は)

____

B **A** の英文 (1) ～ (3) を、適切な空所 (a) ～ (c) に入れて会話を完成しなさい。 CD 63

W: I remember the young man clearly. He was sitting next to me on a flight to London. "(a)" the flight attendant asked him.

M: So what happened then?

W: "Er, er, Coca-Cola, please," he said. (b)

M: Then what?

W: (c)

M: Oh no! That must have really shattered his confidence.

C 質問に対する正しい答えを (A) (B) から選びなさい。

1. What did the flight attendant think the young man was ordering?
   (A) Coca-Cola.　　(B) Coffee.

2. How did the young man probably feel?
   (A) Confident.　　(B) Disappointed.

Grammar　there 構文・使役動詞

There 構文

1. There is [...], There are [...] の使い方

☞ There は形式的な主語で、後続の名詞が意味上の主語
後続の名詞が単数形なら There is、複数形なら There are

There is a good **movie** in the theatre.（その映画館には良い映画があります）

There are some **restaurants** in this street.（この通りにはいくつかのレストランがあります）

2. There is / are の否定文、疑問文

There are no **car parks** near here.（この近くには駐車場がありません）

Are there any **questions** about the lecture?（講演について何かご質問はありますか）

使役動詞の用法

1. 使役動詞 (have, make, let) ＋目的語＋原形不定詞（動詞の原形）

Taking a bath always makes me **feel** good.（風呂に入ることはいつも私を良い気分にしてくれます）

Please let me **know** your plan.（あなたの計画を教えてください）

2. 使役動詞 (get) ＋目的語＋ to 不定詞

I got my friend **to help** me with the itinerary.
（友だちに旅行日程を立てるのを手伝ってもらいました）

3. 使役動詞 (have, get) ＋目的語＋過去分詞

Stella had her car **repaired**.（ステラは車を修理してもらいました）

Unit 26 A Tall Young Man

1 Reading

Yesterday I was sitting in our classroom waiting for the teacher to arrive and to begin teaching our Summer School English course, when a very tall young man sat next to me. "Is this your first day here?" I asked him. When he said it wasn't, I asked how often he came. He said he tried to come and study as often as possible, because he was on a summer-school exchange program from his university in Paris.

I had to ask him about his height. "You look like a basketball player," I said. "How tall are you?" He told me that he was just under two metres and had been a basketball player in school. In fact, he still plays whenever he can, but hasn't got enough time to join a team. "What are you studying in Paris?" I asked. He told me he was majoring in business management.

Wow! Can you imagine this guy in the future when he has graduated from college? His business meeting will have already started, and he will walk in a little late. With his good looks and amazing height, everybody will be stunned. All his proposals will be passed with no trouble, I'm sure.

Notes **a summer-school exchange program**「夏期学生交流プログラム」 **business management**「ビジネスマネージメント、経営学」

1 次の単語の意味を (a) 〜 (e) から選び、下線上にその記号を書きなさい。

1. course _____
2. imagine _____
3. stun _____
4. proposal _____
5. trouble _____

(a) a series of classes on a particular subject
(b) a situation that is difficult or has problems
(c) an idea or suggestion about what should be done
(d) to surprise someone very much
(e) to think of something in your mind

2 次の英文が本文の内容に合っていれば T、違っていれば F を選びなさい。

1. The tall young man is going to begin his studies from today. T F
2. The tall man said he played basketball in school. T F
3. He will always walk into his business meetings on time. T F

2 Conversation

A 会話を聞いて空所に単語を書きなさい。 CD 65

W: Why did you come to this school?
M: It's got $_{1}$(   ) I need.
W: What do you mean?
M: Well, I swim in the pool every day, do weight $_{2}$(   ), and study languages.
W: That must be $_{3}$(   ).
M: Not really. If you live in the city, it is virtually $_{4}$(   ).
W: Really? So I guess that means I am paying too much.

B 質問を聞いて空所に単語を書き、適切な答えを (A) (B) から選びなさい。 CD 66

1. How many (   ) is the man doing?
   (A) Two.   (B) Three.

2. What did the woman (   ) by talking to the young man?
   (A) He seemed to have no interest in swimming.
   (B) He seemed to live in the city.

3 Short Talk

イラストを見ながら、空所に入る単語を語群より選び文章を完成しなさい。

big
head
low
section
sorts

These two people have all $_{1}$(   ) of trouble in their daily lives. When she goes shopping abroad, most of the clothes are too $_{2}$(   ), so she has to look around the children's $_{3}$(   ) to find the right size. He doesn't have much trouble in most places, but in Japan, he often hits his $_{4}$(   ) on doors that are way too $_{5}$(   ). So I'm afraid he doesn't feel too happy over here.

Unit 27 Reading Your Mind　進行形・現在分詞

Warm-up

次の日本語を参考にして、空所に与えられた文字で始まる単語を書きなさい。

釣り　若者　岩　会話

1. He really is a nice (g　　　　), and if you have a (c　　　　　　) with him for a while, you will probably like him.
2. He is sitting on the (r　　　　　　) and holding a (f　　　　　　) rod.

1 Reading

CD 67

My English teacher has been (ア) me to be careful when I talk to others. She says that I am not supposed to ask personal questions or make remarks that might hurt people's feelings. With all these cautions, what can I ask? If I really spoke my mind, what would it sound like? Like this, maybe "Hello Barbara. [*Are you putting on weight?*] Hey, you are (イ) great. [*But your cheeks are very red.*] [①]"

"[*The other day I'm sure I saw you in town, and not with your husband but in a bar with a young and handsome man.*] What have you been up to recently? [*You are looking your age.*] What an interesting dress you are (ウ)! [*I wouldn't be seen dead in that thing. It looks like* [1]*it came from a secondhand market stall.*] Are you still (エ) that old red car? It's a great car. [②] Is that a new hairstyle? [2]It makes you look twenty years younger. [③]"

"I chatted with your husband in the train the other day. He is such an amusing man. [*He talked non-stop all the way home about* (a)(*his work / how / interesting / is*)]. Well, Barbara, (b)(it / lovely / talking / to / was) you. [*We must never do it again.*] Here is my business card. [*But please, don't call.*]"

Notes　**make remarks**「発言をする」　**speak one's mind**「自分の思っていることをはっきり言う」　**put on weight**「太る」　**wouldn't been seen dead**「絶対ごめんだ」　**secondhand market stall**「中古商品を売る屋台、古着屋の屋台」

1 進行形の英文になるように、drive, look, tell, wear のどれかの形を変えて入れなさい。

ア. (　　　　　)　イ. (　　　　　)　ウ. (　　　　　)　エ. (　　　　　)

2 相手の気持ちを害する次の発言が文中の①〜③のどれに入るか答えなさい。

1. [*It is about time you went to a new hairdresser.*]　(　　)
2. [*Are you drinking again?*]　(　　)
3. [*Can't you afford to buy a nicer car?*]　(　　)

3 下線部 1 の it の示す内容を日本語で答えなさい。

4 下線部 2 の It の示す内容を日本語で答えなさい。

5 次の文中の単語と同じ意味の語を (a) 〜 (e) から選びなさい。

1. hurt (　　)　2. caution (　　)　3. handsome (　　)　4. recently (　　)　5. chat (　　)

(a) care　(b) good-looking　(c) harm　(d) lately　(e) talk

6 次の語の下線部の発音と同じ発音の語をア〜エから選びなさい。

1. remark	ア. award	イ. garden	ウ. toward	エ. war
2. stall	ア. access	イ. bath	ウ. mall	エ. racket
3. great	ア. break	イ. idea	ウ. leather	エ. please

7 本文の内容に合うように、空所に与えられた文字で始まる文中の単語を書きなさい。

1. Be careful not to hurt (p　　　　　) feelings when you ask questions.
2. I saw you in a (b　　　　　) in town with a young and handsome man the other day.
3. You can't buy a new (c　　　　　), because you don't have enough money these days.

8 (a) (b) の語句を正しく並べ替えなさい。

(a) (his work / how / interesting / is)

(b) (it / lovely / talking / to / was)

2 Conversation

A 日本文を参考にして（　）の語を正しく並べ替えなさい。ただし文頭に来る語も小文字にしてある。

1. (do / I / think / you / who) saw in town the other day drinking in a bar?
（先日私が、町のバーで誰がお酒を飲んでいるのを見たと思いますか）

2. (do / mean / you / what)?（どういう意味ですか）

3. Yes, (I'm / it / she / sure / was).（いいえ、絶対に彼女でした）

B **A** の英文 (1) ～ (3) を、適切な空所 (a) ～ (c) に入れて会話を完成しなさい。 CD 68

W: (a)
M: No, no, no. Not Barbara!
W: (b)
M: Well, that would explain it.
W: (c)
M: She has been wearing very fashionable clothes recently, and also a lot of makeup.

C 質問に対する正しい答えを (A) (B) から選びなさい。

1. Where was Barbara seen?
   (A) In a bar.　　(B) In the train.

2. What has happened to Barbara recently?
   (A) Nothing at all. She is the same as always.
   (B) She has changed her appearance.

Grammar　進行形・現在分詞

進行形の用法

・be 動詞＋ -ing（現在分詞）

1. 現在・過去・完了・未来の進行している動作

Jessica is watching a movie on TV now.
（ジェシカは今テレビで映画を見ているところです）
When I called, John was having dinner.
（電話をかけたとき、ジョンはディナーを食べているところでした）
Claire has been practicing for the presentation from this morning.
（クレアは今朝からプレゼンテーションの練習をしています）
Ryan will be waiting for me at 3 p.m.（ライアンは午後 3 時に私を待っているでしょう）

2. 近い未来

Olivia is leaving for Boston.（オリビアはボストンに向かう予定です）
Our train is departing in half an hour.（列車は 30 分後に発車します）

現在分詞の作り方

1. 基本は動詞の原形に [-ing]	play → playing	walk → walking
2. [e] で終わる語は [e] を取って [-ing]	use → using	write → writing
3. 短母音＋子音で終わる語は最後の子音字を重ねて [-ing]	run → running	sit → sitting
4. [ie] で終わる語は [-ying]	die → dying	lie → lying
5. [c] で終わる語は [-king]	picnic → picnicking	panic → panicking

Unit 28 I lost my camera.

1 Reading

15 CD 69

I had spent a couple of years saving up all the loose change around the house. By themselves those coins were not valuable ... one yen here, five yen there. But this "coin mountain" had now matured, and I was able to buy the camera I had long been dreaming of. Now, I was on my way home. I was on the train, sitting excitedly on a bench seat with my camera next to me in a box. I was deciding what kind of photos to take first of all. But then I realised that next to me was an empty space. There was no box and no camera.

I took a train back to the terminal station in the city and walked into the station office on the platform. My voice was trembling. "Excuse me, please. I lost my camera earlier this morning. I think I forgot it in this station. I sat on one of those blue bench seats over there for about ten minutes, and then got on the express train when it came in." The station manager said, "Well, this is your lucky day. The cleaning lady found a camera on the floor, under that bench, just a few minutes ago. It must have been there for half an hour. Now then, can you fill in this form with your name and address, and then describe your camera? When you have done that, you can take it home."

Notes **save up**「貯める」 **loose change**「小銭」 **station office**「駅務室」 **express train**「急行列車」 **station manager**「駅長」 **This is your lucky day.**「今日はついていますね」 **fill in**「記入する」

1 次の単語の意味を (a) ～ (e) から選び、下線上にその記号を書きなさい。

1. valuable _____
2. mature _____
3. terminal _____
4. tremble _____
5. describe _____

(a) a place where trains start and finish
(b) to become fully developed
(c) to tell what something is like
(d) to shake slightly because you are nervous
(e) worth a lot of money

2 次の英文が本文の内容に合っていれば T、違っていれば F を選びなさい。

1. The man was able to buy a camera because he was given a big bonus. T F
2. Before he got on the train, he sat on a bench seat on the platform. T F
3. He was lucky because a kind passenger found the camera. T F

2 Conversation

A 会話を聞いて空所に単語を書きなさい。 CD 70

M: I started photography when I was a kid.

W: What sort of $_{1}$( ) did you take?

M: Pictures of steam trains. I thought they were beautiful monsters of $_{2}$( ).

W: What $_{3}$( ) now?

M: Mainly people.

W: Do you work in a studio?

M: Yes, but I also $_{4}$( ) taking pictures of vehicles such as cars and trains.

B 質問を聞いて空所に単語を書き、適切な答えを (A) (B) から選びなさい。 CD 71

1. What was his main theme when he ( ) photography?
   (A) People. (B) Steam trains.

2. What is his ( ) now?
   (A) People. (B) Pets.

3 Short Talk

イラストを見ながら、空所に入る単語を語群より選び文章を完成しなさい。

get
keep
lap
off
seeing

Life is a survival game. Of course, if you lose your camera, you want to $_{1}$( ) it back. If you want a chance of $_{2}$( ) your camera again, you had better $_{3}$( ) the receipt and write down the camera's body and lens numbers. I didn't do any of these things today. I went to a coffee shop. I took $_{4}$( ) my gloves when I made a phone call. On the train on the way home, I put my daypack on my $_{5}$( ) and set my camera next to me. I am a lucky person if my camera is still here.

Unit 29 In the Police Box 受動態・仮定法

Warm-up

次の日本語を参考にして、空所に与えられた文字で始まる単語を書きなさい。

浅い　アナウンス　ビーチ　テント

1. On the (b　　　　) my daughter was playing in the sand.
2. I had no worries, because the water there is very (s　　　　).
3. I told her to remember where our (t　　　　) was, and off she went.
4. Later, I heard an (a　　　　　　) that a little child had got lost.

1 Reading

CD 72

I know you are not going to believe this, but what happened to me might happen to you. I [ア](will / would) have driven to town [イ](if / without) my car had been available. But it ①(use) by my brother for the day, and so Grandma and [1]I took the train into town. We got there without any trouble and looked around the station shops. I had to go to the toilet, so I told Grandma to sit and wait for me. But when I came out, I couldn't find her anywhere. [2]I went to the police box, and the young policeman there said, "Yes, madam, can I help you?" I answered, "Well, I know it sounds silly, but my grandmother ②(lose) and so has to ③(find)."

"Can you describe her?" he asked [ウ](as though / despite of) my problem was nothing out of the ordinary. "Well, she is in her 80s," I said. "She's quite short, and today she's wearing a grey skirt and a blue top. She's very friendly and is always talking to people. She thinks everyone is her son or daughter, [(a)](follows / people / she / so) everywhere." He said, "Right, I've got [3]that. Now then, [(b)](did / her / lose / where / you)?" "At the station," I told him. But now the Station Café staff have just contacted me. They said that an elderly woman who never stops talking is waiting for me to come and get her.

Notes **nothing out of the ordinary**「日常の出来事」 **top**「トップス、上着」 **I've got that.**「わかりました」

1 仮定法にするため、ア～ウの適切な語句を選びなさい。

ア. (　　　　　　　　) イ. (　　　　　　　　) ウ. (　　　　　　　　)

2 ①～③の単語を受動態になるように適切な形にしなさい。

① (　　　　　　　　　　) ② (　　　　　　　　　　) ③ (　　　　　　　　　　)

3 次の単語の下線部の発音と同じ発音の語をア～エから選びなさい。

1. describe	ア. decision	イ. pick	ウ. police	エ. tide
2. quite	ア. cruise	イ. recruit	ウ. require	エ. suitable
3. lose	ア. folk	イ. improve	ウ. woman	エ. wonderful

4 指示に従って書き換えなさい。

1. 下線部 1 を否定文に

2. 下線部 2 で the police box を問う疑問文に

5 下線部 3 の that が表す具体的な内容を日本語で書きなさい。

6 本文の内容に合うように、空所に与えられた文字で始まる文中の単語を書きなさい。

1. Grandma was told to sit and wait because the woman had gone to the (t　　　　　　).
2. At the (s　　　　　　) the woman found that Grandma was missing.
3. The (p　　　　　　) didn't seem to be surprised about the news.

7 (a) (b) の語を正しく並べ替えなさい。

(a) (follows / people / she / so)

(b) (did / her / lose / where / you)

2 Conversation

A 日本文を参考にして（　）の語句を正しく並べ替えなさい。文頭に来るものも小文字にしてある。

1. But I couldn't (do / how / it / remember / to).
（しかし、どうしたらいいか思い出すことができませんでした）

2. Yes, I remember that. (a / in / it / notebook / was). （はい、覚えています。手帳にありました）

3. I (and / my ID / her / she / showed) wrote it for me.（私は身分証明書を見せ、彼女が書きました）

B **A** の英文 (1) ～ (3) を、適切な空所 (a) ～ (c) に入れて会話を完成しなさい。 CD 73

M: Somewhere I wrote that I don't want to wear an ID round my neck.

W: (a)

M: Well, I think I am changing my mind. Yesterday I went to the post office, and the young assistant asked me to write my address. (b)

W: So what did you do?

M: (c)

W: I wonder how many people like you she gets every day?

C 質問に対する正しい答えを (A) (B) から選びなさい。

1. What was the man's problem at the post office?
   (A) He had forgotten his reading glasses.
   (B) He had forgotten how to write his address.

2. What is he now ready to accept?
   (A) That he should not walk around alone.
   (B) That he should wear an ID.

Grammar　受動態・仮定法

受動態

・be 動詞＋過去分詞＋ (by)

1. 能動態と受動態の書き換え

He **reached** the city hall.（彼は市役所に着きました）
The city hall was reached by him.

I **will meet** my cousin at the station.（私は駅でいとこに会うでしょう）
My cousin will be met by me at the station.

She **is carrying** the suitcase.（彼女はスーツケースを運んでいます）
The suitcase is being carried by her.

2. by 以外の前置詞

Mickey Mouse is known **to** everyone.（ミッキーマウスはみんなに知られています）

仮定法

1. 仮定法過去：現在の事実に反することの仮定

☞ If ＋ 主語 ＋ 過去形，主語 ＋ could (would, might, should) ＋ 動詞の原形

If he had computer skills, he could get a good job.
(コンピュータ操作技能があれば、彼は良い仕事を得られるでしょう)

2. 仮定法過去完了：過去の事実に反することの仮定

☞ If ＋ 主語 ＋ had ＋ 過去分詞，主語 ＋ could (would, might, should) ＋ have ＋ 過去分詞

If she had had more time, she could have finished the report.
(もっと時間があったら、彼女はレポートを書き終えることができたでしょう)

3. 仮定法の慣用的表現

Without your advice, I **wouldn't have studied** abroad.
(あなたのアドバイスがなければ、私は留学しなかったでしょう)

He speaks English as if he **were** a native speaker.（彼はまるでネイティブのように英語を話します）

Unit 30 Studying English

1 Reading

16 CD 74

People often ask me what the best way to learn English is. Maybe they are searching for a magical method and an easy way to learn. However, my answer is to look for something different — I mean, a really effective approach to learning. For me, learning is fun, free, and exciting. If you believe that, teaching and studying are not really your jobs. Instead they are like your hobbies.

That kind of approach to language learning changes your whole life. Finding something new such as a new word or a way of saying something is as exciting as a visit from Santa. You don't need a big reward each day, however. Something small now and then is good enough to keep you pleased. When will you stop learning English and say enough is enough? Some students aim to get a high exam score, because after that, they won't have to study English any more. Other students look for ways to keep using English.

By talking and sharing information, people become happy. So why don't you look for a job that you can use English at? Perhaps your life will become fun, and your business will succeed.

Notes **now and then**「時々」 **enough is enough**「もうたくさんだ」 **not ... any more**「もう〜ない」

1 次の単語の意味を (a) 〜 (e) から選び、下線上にその記号を書きなさい。

1. magical _____
2. approach _____
3. reward _____
4. please _____
5. aim _____

(a) a way of thinking about or doing something
(b) full of mystery and excitement
(c) something received in return for doing something good
(d) to have a goal or purpose
(e) to make someone happy or satisfied

2 次の英文が本文の内容に合っていれば T、違っていれば F を選びなさい。

1. If you enjoy learning, it becomes like a hobby. T F
2. Santa often comes to the man's house to teach English. T F
3. Combining work and language learning can make you happy. T F

2 Conversation

A 会話を聞いて空所に単語を書きなさい。 CD 75

W: How did you learn Japanese, which is very good, by the way?

M: Because I lived in Japan, I was able to listen to Japanese in action while in the train, say, or out $_1$(　　　　　　).

W: What exactly do you mean by “Japanese in action”?

M: Young kids, teenagers, and adults all use $_2$(　　　　　　) kinds of Japanese. So I just listened to them — and learned from them.

W: Is there any $_3$(　　　　　　) with such a learning method?

M: Well, I didn’t have a teacher, so I guess my learning lacked a real $_4$(　　　　　　).

W: Well, I don’t live in the US or the UK, so I’ll just have to listen to English on TV more!

B 質問を聞いて空所に単語を書き、適切な答えを (A) (B) から選びなさい。 CD 76

1. Where was the man’s Japanese “(　　　　　　　　)”?
   (A) At school.　　　(B) Out in public with people.

2. What learning (　　　　　　) will the woman use?
   (A) She will listen to English on TV.
   (B) She will move to the UK.

3 Short Talk

イラストを見ながら、空所に入る単語を語群より選び文章を完成しなさい。

dishes
from
talking
time
used

How did I learn Japanese? Of course, my TV was my teacher. The people on TV often $_1$(　　　　　　) the same phrases over and over, and so I was able to pick up the language $_2$(　　　　　　) them. I also listened to people $_3$(　　　　　　) in the supermarket or in the train, and so my ears became like radar $_4$(　　　　　　). It took a long $_5$(　　　　　　) to learn Japanese, but it was fun.

English Here and There

by
Terry O'Brien
Kei Mihara
Tadashi Enya
Hiroshi Kimura

English Here and There [B-907]
読解と基本文法で極める総合英語

1刷　2020年 1月 29日

著　者	テリー・オブライエン	Terry O'Brien
	三原　京	Kei Mihara
	塩谷　直史	Tadashi Enya
	木村　博是	Hiroshi Kimura

発行者　南雲　一範　Kazunori Nagumo
発行所　株式会社　南雲堂
〒162-0801　東京都新宿区山吹町361
NAN'UN-DO Co., Ltd.
361 Yamabuki-cho, Shinjuku-ku, Tokyo 162-0801, Japan
振替口座 : 00160-0-46863
TEL: 03-3268-2311（営業部：学校関係）
03-3268-2384（営業部：書店関係）
03-3268-2387（編集部）
FAX: 03-3269-2486

編集者　加藤　敦
製　版　橋本　佳子
装　丁　Nスタジオ
検　印　省　略
コード　ISBN978-4-523-17907-8　C0082

Printed in Japan

E-mail　nanundo@post.email.ne.jp
URL　http://www.nanun-do.co.jp/